CHICAGO'S GREATEST BUILDINGS

Skyscrapers, Landmarks, and Hidden Gems in the City of Architecture

Ellen Shubart

REEDY PRESS

DEDICATION

As always, to my family. No matter where you live, think of Chicago as home.

Reedy Press
PO Box 5131
St. Louis, MO, 63139, USA
reedypress.com

Design by Richard Roden
All photos by Richard Wald Shubart

LOC: 2025943577
ISBN: 9781681066035

Printed in Canada
25 26 27 28 29 5 4 3 2 1

CONTENTS

Northeastern Illinois University El Centro Campus

INTRODUCTION

Chicago is the City of Architecture, and we are as proud of our 21st-century glass-clad skyscrapers as we are of their historic precursors, always celebrating our evolving skyline. Chicago is the birthplace of the skyscraper, the place where architects forged an American style, and where their experiments with new technologies and designs resulted in buildings that reach to the skies.

Creating a list of Chicago's greatest buildings is obviously subjective. Yet, in selecting these buildings the criteria almost built (pardon the pun) themselves. Appended adjectives explain their inclusion: "first," "tallest," "largest," "best example of." Others played a significant role in the city's history.

Are they all skyscrapers? Emphatically no!

Are they all downtown? No to that, too. These buildings are spread throughout the city, although logically most are in the greater downtown Loop.

But they are all secular buildings. No churches, monuments, parks, or sites are included—each of these categories could be a book unto itself. And all are within the city. So much wonderful architecture exists outside city limits that inclusion of one would require the addition of too many.

The selection includes works by the best-known architects affiliated with Chicago—from Daniel Burnham, Louis Sullivan, and William Le Baron Jenney in the 19th century to Ludwig Mies van der Rohe, Jeanne Gang, and Adrian Smith of more contemporary times—plus architects with worldwide reputations who contributed one or more designs to Chicago: Rafael Viñoly, Sir Norman Foster, and Rem Koolhaas.

Taken together, these structures illustrate the glory of Chicago architecture—from the small water tower left standing after the horrendous 1871 fire to today's towering, sustainably designed buildings.

The "greatest" is certainly in the eye of the beholder. These are my choices. Please enjoy them with me—a collection suited to a city that revels in its architecture.

Marina City

ACKNOWLEDGMENTS

As always, I have to thank my husband, Richard, for all his hard work in taking the pictures, copyediting, and going around with me to find all these buildings that reside in Chicago. Richard is an intrepid explorer and has been for all of my books.

I also have to profusely thank my friend Kathleen Carpenter, responsible for making the architectural details and jargon translatable for a general public audience. She is fabulous, and I can't say enough to thank her. Many of the great architectural insights are hers; any errors, of course, are mine.

In researching this book, I came to realize the gigantic and superior job that is done by the American Institute of Architects Chicago and its editor, Laurie McGovern Petersen, in creating the *AIA Guide to Chicago*. We in Chicago are so lucky to have such an intrepid historian to chronicle our built environment. I had to select only 82 buildings; she reports on thousands.

I could not have written a book like this 15 years ago; my volunteer gig as a Chicago Architecture Center docent, leading tours, has given me the knowledge and the research capability to do so. Being a docent is rewarding in so many ways and has made my retirement a continuous learning experience.

Thanks, too, to the Reedy Press team, from Josh Stevens and Barbara Northcott on down. It is always a pleasure to work with this team.

135 SOUTH LASALLE STREET

(FIELD BUILDING)

1934: Graham, Anderson, Probst & White, Alfred P. Shaw, architect

This excellent representative of the vertical Art Deco style with a spectacular lobby shows off then-new 1930s skyscraper technology. But, perhaps ironically, it was the last major skyscraper built in Chicago before the Depression and World War II.

The steel-framed building's four side towers go 22 stories high, with a central tower that is 43 stories high. Clad in Indiana limestone, with a black granite base, identical entrances exist on both LaSalle and Clark Streets, each doorway five stories high for the building that spans a city block.

Inside, a two-level, block-long lobby is done in the Jazz Age's preferred Art Deco style, sleek with cream-colored mosaic terrazzo floors, cream-white marble on the walls, and recessed panels of beige Italian marble, with rich nickel silver metalwork adding to the glamour. Overhead, mirrored bridges link the north and south balconies. Imagine the steamship era and 1930s movie stars Fred Astaire and Ginger Rogers gliding down the long hall, gazing up at the Cartier-inspired timepieces, and you've got the picture. Midway off the lobby were state-of-the-art high-speed elevators, the largest elevator bank (42 elevators) in any Chicago office building, with an elevator indicator that is a mini replica of the building.

The building developers, the Field family, descendants of retail mogul Marshall Field, included many new amenities: a central vacuum system, chilled water fountains in every suite, and most remarkably, air-conditioning up to the fifth floor.

The site formerly held the William Le Baron Jenney–designed Home Insurance Building, sometimes called America's first skyscraper. It was demolished in 1931 for the Field Building.

Designated a Chicago landmark in 1994, the building was included in June 2013 in the West Loop–LaSalle Street Historic District on the National Register of Historic Places. Today, some of the upper floors are being converted to residential living.

BANK OF AMERICA

13'-10"
E Ida B. Wells Dr
500 S
ROBERT
MORRIS
CENTER
ROBERT
MORRIS
CENTER

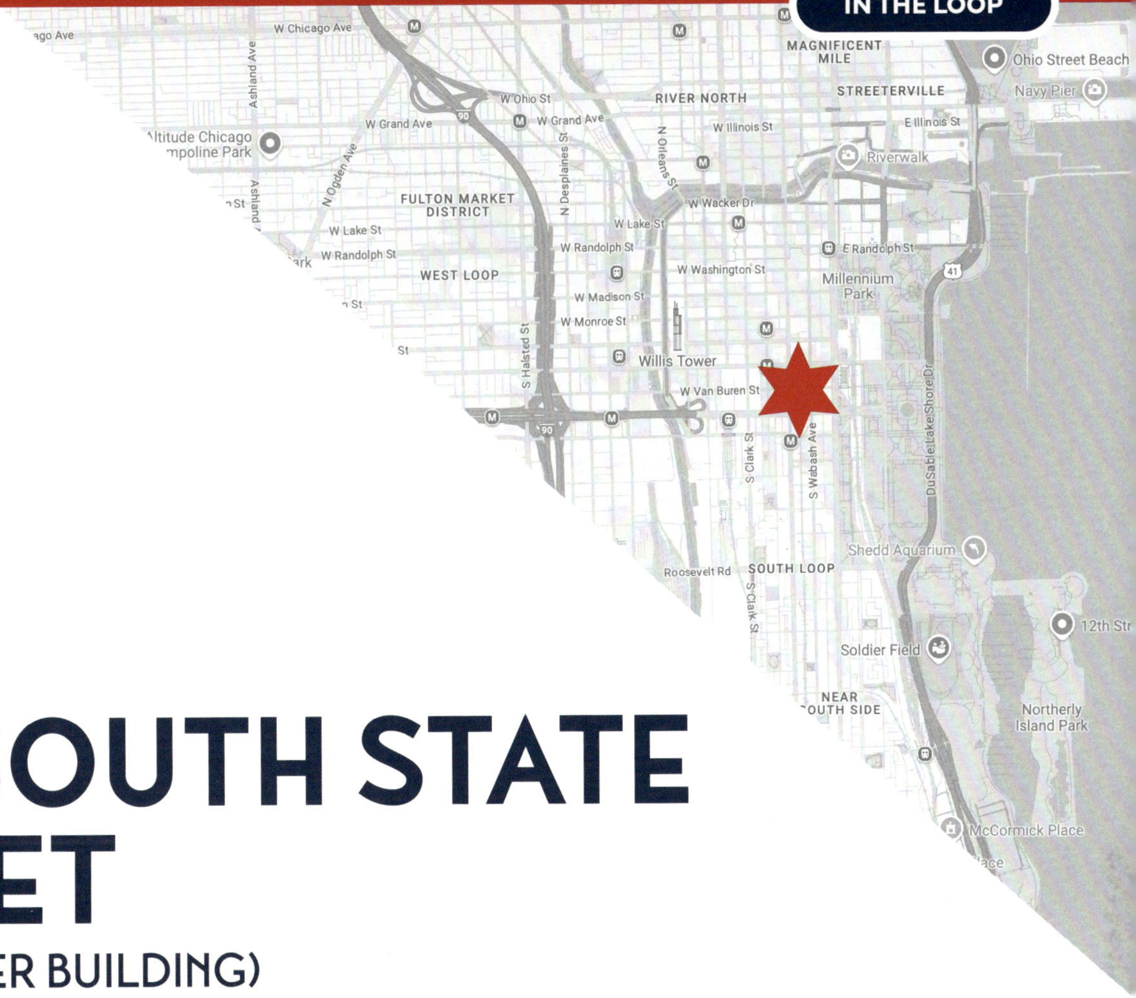

403 SOUTH STATE STREET

(SECOND LEITER BUILDING)

1891: William Le Baron Jenney

The Second Leiter Building began life as one of the earliest and best examples of a steel-frame warehouse/retail store. The building is huge, with spaciousness unequaled for the time and suitable for the then-new retail emporiums rising along State Street.

The eight-story building fills an entire block with 553,000 square feet, an accomplishment for the day. The interior featured wide-open floors for maximum sales space. Retailers could display goods with illuminating outside light, and the thin wrought-iron support columns didn't interfere. The unusually wide window bays and high ceilings added to the spaciousness. Sears, Roebuck & Co. operated its flagship retail store here for 46 years.

Building developer Levi Leiter was a former partner of Marshall Field. He sought a retail establishment with lots of space, and architect William Le Baron Jenney delivered. Jenney was the master of steel framing. His Civil War work in the Union Army was designing bridges.

Using his experience and applying it to buildings, Jenney has often been credited with designing the world's first skyscraper, the Home Insurance Co. Whether it was first or not, Jenney takes credit for developing the concept of steel-frame construction, which meant buildings would no longer be held up by their outer masonry walls, but instead would rest on a frame of steel or iron.

Jenney also was a mentor to most of the major Chicago architects a generation younger, including Daniel Burnham, Louis Sullivan, William Holabird, and Martin Roche, all of whom began their careers in Jenney's office.

The building was named both to the National Register of Historic Places and as a National Historic Landmark in January 1996. One year later it was declared a Chicago Landmark. The building is currently owned by Roosevelt University.

820 South Michigan Avenue

820 SOUTH
(JOHNSON PUBLISHING COMPANY)

1971: Dubin, Dubin, Black & Moutoussamy

The first and only downtown skyscraper designed by a Black architect, this building began as headquarters for Johnson Publishing Co., the firm behind the nationally circulated *Ebony* and *Jet* magazines. Architect John Warren Moutoussamy was a pioneering architect, the first Black person to make partner at a majority-white Chicago architecture firm. As such, the 11-story structure plays a major role in Chicago's Black history.

Johnson Publishing utilized the building for 45 years. In the 1970s, when the company moved downtown, it was the second-largest African American business in the US; by the 1980s, it was the largest.

After serving in World War II, Chicagoan Moutoussamy studied under famed Modernist Ludwig Mies van der Rohe at the Illinois Institute of Technology (today, Illinois Tech). Owner John Johnson said he "did not want one of those 'shirt front' glass and steel buildings." Instead, he requested a unique building that would convey his company's "openness to truth . . . to light . . . to all currents swirling in all the black communities of this land."

The building displays its structure, with columns set in from the side walls. Recessed banded windows look out at Grant Park and Lake Michigan. Originally clad in travertine, later replaced with granite, the building had open floor plans and an absence of ornament.

When it was sold by Johnson Publishing, the first purchaser, Chicago's Columbia College, wanted to renovate it for a college library. But that plan was scuttled due to both cost and changes in library science, which emphasized digital materials, not space for books.

Acquired by 3L Real Estate in 2017, the building has been converted into a 150-apartment residence. A new addition and roof deck were added, and an iconic "Ebony JP Jet" sign on the rooftop was restored.

The building was designated a Chicago Landmark in November 2017.

FOR LEASE

200 East Randolph Street

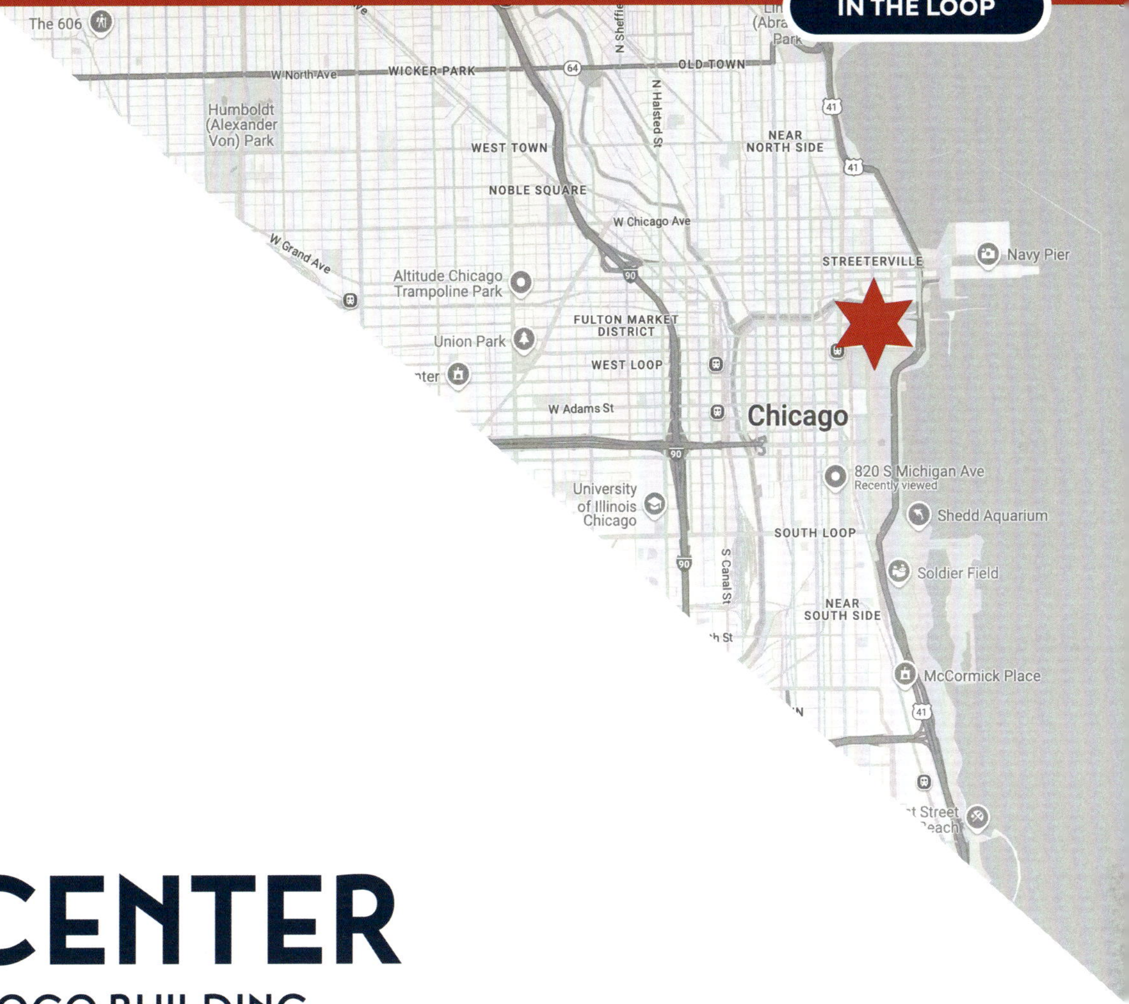

AON CENTER

(FORMERLY AMOCO BUILDING, ORIGINALLY STANDARD OIL BUILDING)

1973: Edward Durell Stone; Perkins & Will, associate architects

The Aon Center would have been Chicago's tallest building were it not for the Sears/Willis Tower, which opened in the same year, 1973. Today, the white-granite-clad building stands as only the fourth tallest in the city.

A different take on Modernism, the design of Aon was a departure from the dark steel and glass that was so popular in the 1960s and '70s. The 93-story building is basically a long, hollow tube. Perimeter columns holding utility lines allow for column-free interior floors. The dark tint of the windows contrasts strongly with the white sheathing, and the columns emphasize verticality in the design.

The Aon has been called "the building built twice." Originally clad in Italian white Carrara marble, it had to be reclad in 1990–92 after the thinly sliced marble began to buckle and there were fears of falling stone. Chicago's freeze-thaw winters are hard on buildings.

After the 43,000 marble panels were removed, the building was reclad in North Carolina granite, which is also white but much stronger against the winter weather. The cost was $80 million, more than half the cost of the original construction of $120 million. The new white cladding has a matte finish rather than a glossy one. The 6,000 tons of removed marble were given new life in the form of bookends, trophies, and paperweights—often given to retiring Standard Oil workers—or ground up as road base.

Renovations of the plazas surrounding the building were undertaken in 2021, with an aim at making the building more easily accessible and desirable for rentals.

A promised observatory and sky-high thrill ride from the rooftop have never materialized.

225 NORTH COLUMBUS DRIVE

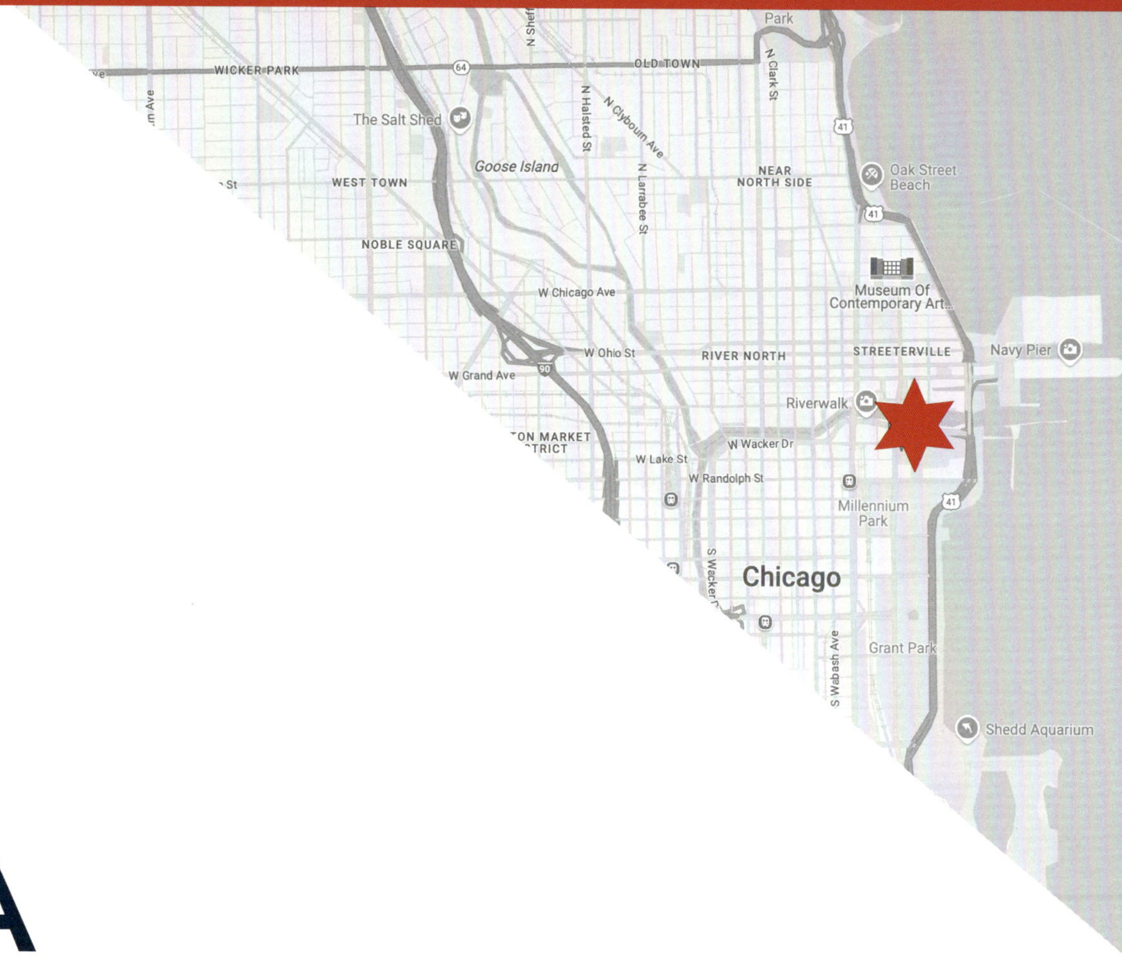

AQUA

2009: Studio Gang, Jeanne Gang, lead designer; Loewenberg Architects, architect of record

This building knocks your socks off—and has been praised for doing so since it opened. It is "one of the most audacious and photographic high-rises in the city," says architecture critic Vladimir Belogolovsky.

Aqua was the first of the many new Lakeshore East neighborhood buildings to literally sparkle with 21st-century innovation. Architect Jeanne Gang created a stir with the building's undulating balconies and striking facades that mimic falling water and ponds.

The mixed-use 87-story building has 263 condominium residences on the upper floors (53–82), 474 rental apartments on the middle floors (19–52), and a Radisson Blu–branded hotel, the first Blu in the US, filling the lower 18 stories.

It is the balconies that draw the "ohs" of admiration. Each is unique, providing residents with unusual views and giving them different sizes of outdoor balcony space, ranging from 12 feet in depth in some places to only one foot elsewhere. While the undulating patterns are visually impressive, they also protect the building from heavy winds and provide sun shade to many units, particularly in the summer. The dark gray aluminum balcony railings are open metalwork, allowing interactions among high-in-the-sky neighbors similar to those on a traditional neighborhood stoop, something Gang encourages. The balconies and the reflective, treated glass on the facades prevent birds from flying into the building.

Retail space fronts Columbus Drive, on the building's western side, and facing the six-acre Lakeshore East Park on the east are nine townhouses, which together hide a large three-story garage. An 80,000-square-foot roof garden filled with amenities includes a running track and swimming pool, designed by landscape architect Ted Wolff.

In a plethora of glass and steel high-rises, Aqua could visually get lost. But its beauty and unique design stand out. Simply put, it is a stunner.

407 South Dearborn Street

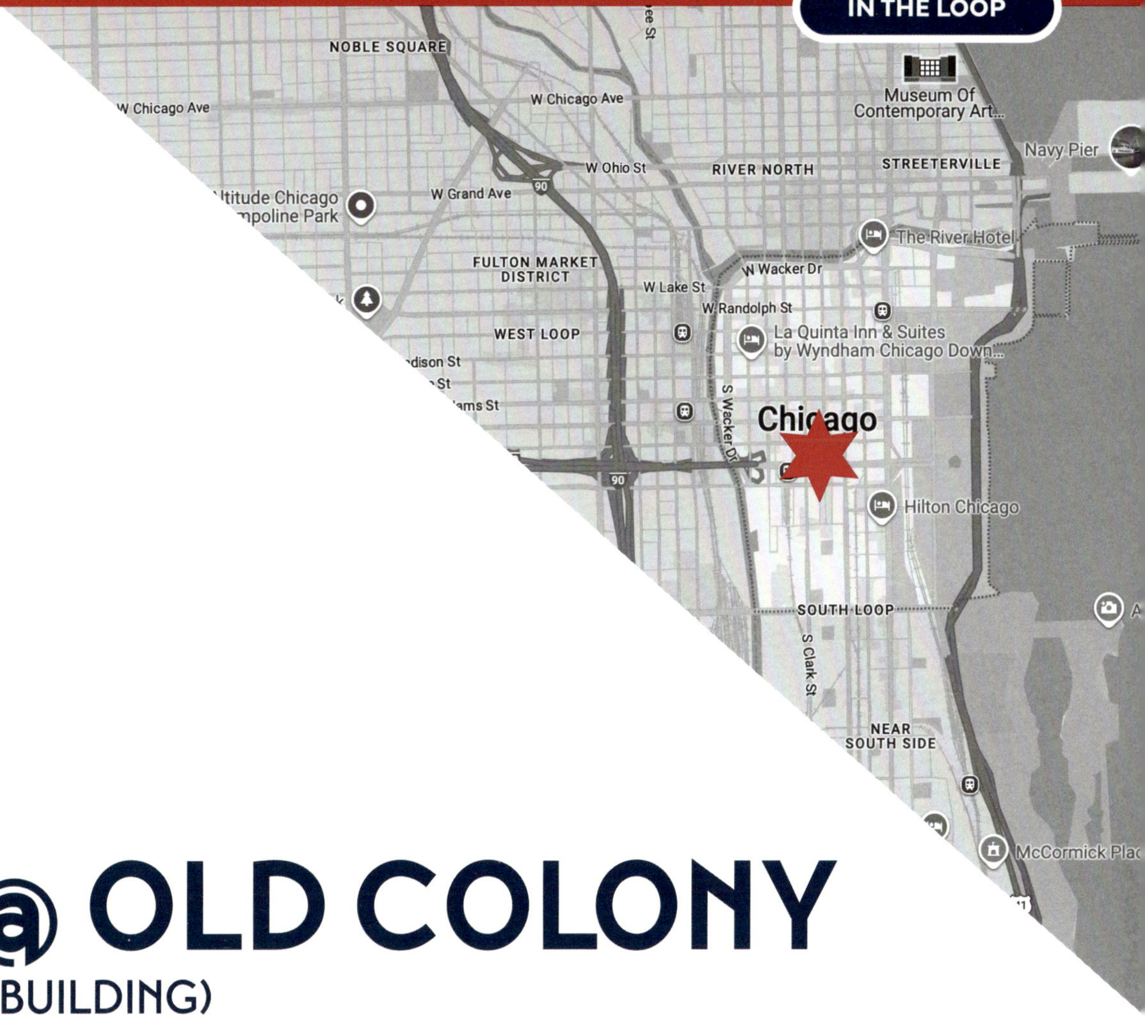

ARC @ OLD COLONY

(OLD COLONY BUILDING)

1893-4: Holabird & Roche

A tall office building that almost becomes invisible because it sits next to the raised tracks of the "L," Chicago's elevated transit system, this is the sole survivor of what were called rounded-cornered Chicago School skyscrapers.

The building has a steel structure, reaching 17 stories. The beautifully decorated oriel windows provide bays along the length of the building on Dearborn Street and beautiful corners on the Van Buren Street front. Oriels are windows that project from the building's main wall but do not reach the ground.

Rounded corners, which rise from the third story to the cornice, were once common devices used to create both desirable large corner offices on the interior—some with as much as 13-foot interior diameters—and interesting exterior silhouettes.

A typical Chicago School–style building, the Old Colony is divided into three parts: a three-story Indiana limestone base; an 11-story shaft in cream-colored Roman brick and terra-cotta; and at the top, three stories of white terra-cotta with a colonnade on the 15th and 16th stories, topped by an overhanging decorative cornice. Terra-cotta is clay baked in a mold at high temperatures for days; it is fire-resistant. Old Colony was one of the first buildings to include interior wind bracing and fireproofed walls.

Old Colony was named for Plymouth, the first English colony in America, whose seal is carved above the entrances.

While for years a successful office building, in 2015 the Old Colony was adaptively repurposed into apartment units. It is currently a privately owned residence hall for students who attend many of the surrounding universities.

Old Colony was designated a Chicago Landmark in 1978, entered on the National Register of Historic Places also in 1978, and is part of the 1976 National Historic Landmark Dearborn Printing House Row District.

MICHIGAN AVENUE AT ADAMS STREET

ART INSTITUTE OF CHICAGO

(1893 BUILDING)

1893: Shepley, Rutan & Coolidge

Chicago's art museum, one of the nation's oldest and largest, was founded in 1879 and quickly outgrew its space. This grand building was erected in 1893, used first as a conference center for the 1893 World's Columbian Exposition (Fair), then turned over to the Art Institute of Chicago (AIC) for a permanent home.

An exemplar of the fair's architectural style, French-inspired Beaux Arts, it was the city's first permanent building to show off Beaux Arts' Neo-Classical forms and light colors. It "signaled," one critic wrote, "Chicago's arrival among the great cities of the world."

The massive, symmetrical building faces Michigan Avenue. The masonry load-bearing walls, without steel support, are made of rusticated (unpolished) limestone on the first level and smooth limestone above. A series of colonnades parade across the second story. Friezes of Greek figures are close to the roofline, and above them march the names of world-famous artists, many of whose works would not be included in the collection until years later. A huge triangle with corner accents—in architectural parlance a pediment with acroteria—tops the entrance.

With a large and comprehensive art collection anchored by Impressionist art donated by the 1890s Chicago society doyenne Bertha Palmer, the AIC became one of the nation's leading art museums. Needing additional space as it grew, the AIC and its school fill this building plus eight additions.

Standing proudly in front are Chicago's "mascots," two larger-than-life bronze lion statues by sculptor Edward Kemeys. They are not identical; north of the main stairway the lion is "on the prowl," and on the south is "in an attitude of defiance." The lions wear sports gear when any Chicago team wins a national title—rarely seen in recent years—and sport wreaths to celebrate the holiday season.

In February 2002, the building was included in the city's Historic Michigan Boulevard Landmark District.

THE ART INSTITVTE OF CHICAGO
PROJECT A BLACK PLANET
THE ART AND CULTURE OF PANAFRICA

201 East Monroe Street

ART INSTITUTE OF CHICAGO: MODERN WING

2009: Renzo Piano Building Workshop, design architects; Interactive Design Architects, architect of record

The Modern Wing, the newest and largest addition to the Art Institute of Chicago, by Pritzker Architecture Prize winner Renzo Piano, is clad primarily in white Indiana limestone with a double curtain wall of glass on its northern facade and a "flying carpet" roof cover. It is the carpet, or sunshade, that distinguishes the Modern Wing, which houses the museum's contemporary 20th- and 21st-century art and acts as the building's second entrance.

The overwhelming theme here is light. Providing natural light inside an art museum is a 21st-century innovation made possible by, among other factors, changes in the composition of glass. The sunshade floats on thin steel columns, overhanging the building. Its curving, moveable aluminum blades screen out direct sunlight, allowing soft, natural light into third-floor galleries. That is augmented by the light that flows in from the glass wall of the entry atrium.

Situated on the southwest corner of Columbus Drive and Monroe Street, the 240,000-square-foot building is linked to its across-the-street neighbor, Millennium Park. The 620-foot straight brushed aluminum Nichols Bridgeway, an elevated walkway, was added to the museum design when plans for the urban park were unveiled. The bridge reaches into the park a full city block north of Monroe Street.

The building also is a neighbor to a significant architectural relic: the former entrance to the Chicago Stock Exchange building, an 1894 masterpiece by architect Louis Sullivan. It was salvaged when the Chicago Stock Exchange building was demolished.

The three-story Modern Wing has art galleries on the second and third floors, the northern one benefitting most from the sunshade and energy-saving double-layered glass. Looking out, those windows showcase the attention-grabbing views of Millennium Park across the street. The western end of the building hosts a rooftop sculpture garden.

430 SOUTH MICHIGAN AVENUE

AUDITORIUM (THEATRE) BUILDING

1889: Adler & Sullivan

The Auditorium Building, the first major commission for architects Dankmar Adler and Louis Sullivan, celebrates Adler's acoustic and engineering expertise and Sullivan's decorative genius. When it opened, it was the largest building in the US and tallest in Chicago. It marked Chicago's arrival in the world as a cultural center.

The mixed-use building included a 400-room hotel, 136 office spaces, a 17-story tower, and a spectacular more-than-4,000-seat theater. Today, the hotel is gone, the building has been adaptively repurposed as a university, and the theater sparkles after being restored to its original glory.

Adler devised the floating foundation (of rafts) that carries the immense weight of these masonry load-bearing walls, made of rusticated (unpolished) granite on lower levels and Indiana limestone for the rest. He also engineered the hydraulically operated stage and is responsible for the theater's superb acoustics. A spoken word without amplification can be heard from the stage to the top row of seats.

Sullivan, an advocate for an original, organic American architecture, showed off his later-to-be-signature arches at the building's entrances. On the interior, his colorful, stenciled ornamentation and Roman mosaic floors contribute to the building's grandeur, as do murals over the stage proscenium, inglenooks (seating areas) in the balcony lobbies, and magnificent stairways with art glass windows.

Having fallen into disrepair by 1946, the building was purchased by Roosevelt University. The former hotel lobby with its massive Sullivan-designed entry stairwell, second floor loggia, and Ganz Hall music venue were transformed for college use. The former 10th-floor dining room is now a library. The Auditorium Theater Council undertook the theater's restoration, reopening it in 1968.

The Auditorium was named to the National Register of Historic Places in 1970, designated a National Historic Landmark in 1975, and designated a Chicago Landmark in 1976.

CHICAGO ATHLETIC ASSOCIATION
CHICAGO

12 South
Michigan Avenue

CHICAGO ATHLETIC ASSOCIATION HOTEL

(CHICAGO ATHLETIC ASSOCIATION)

1893: Henry Ives Cobb

Architect Henry Ives Cobb created a Venetian vision along Michigan Avenue, aimed at impressing visitors to the 1893 World's Columbian Exposition (Fair). With a design based on the Doge's Palace in Venice, the building front combines columns with artistic windows and arches. No expense was spared inside or out, resulting in one of the most beautiful buildings in the city.

Built for the Chicago Athletic Association, an elite men's club formed in 1890, it provided business leaders with the 19th-century equivalent of a fitness center and social club. It opened just months ahead of the fair with 3,000 members and a 10-year waiting list. Women were allowed only for Wednesday dinners and Sunday afternoon events.

The building is designed in a Venetian-Gothic style, with Venetian S-shaped ogee arches and quatrefoil (like a four-leaf clover) windows combined with Gothic colonnettes, or slim columns. A stone panel below the lower cornice features stylized carvings of lacrosse sticks, balls, and rackets, referring to the building's original use. The entryway shows the club's "C" logo, which should be familiar because in the 1920s, CAA member William Wrigley secured the rights to use it for his new Chicago Cubs baseball team.

In 2015, following a major decline in membership, even after opening the club to women in 1971, the clubhouse was sold. Re-creating the 1890s experience through restoration of most of the superb mosaic floors, art glass windows, and sculptured moldings has been lauded as museum-quality restoration.

Although the building is short, just seven stories, the view from the rooftop—available to visitors to the bar or restaurant—is fabulous. The terrace provides views of the swath of parks and skyscrapers along Lake Michigan.

The building was landmarked in 2002 as a contributing building in the Historic Michigan Boulevard District.

141 West Jackson Boulevard

CHICAGO BOARD OF TRADE

1930: Holabird and Root
1980: Addition: Murphy/Jahn, with Shaw and Associates; Swanke, Hayden, Connell Architects

Standing tall at the end of LaSalle Street, the Chicago Board of Trade Building symbolizes Chicago's economic strength. The CBOT, founded in 1848, celebrates the Midwest's agricultural and financial ties. Fittingly, the building is topped with an elegant 31-foot statue of Ceres, the goddess of grain and harvests—or cereal.

The 45-story limestone structure, designed in the Art Deco style where the eye is pulled upward by strong vertical lines, was, for a time, the tallest in Chicago. Its nine-story base is flanked by two 30-story wings, creating a giant chair shape. The applied ornamentation bespeaks the building's function: agricultural futures trading. Alvin Meyers's sculptures of bovine heads (cattle? sheep?) on one level, together with huge statues of an old-world farmer holding wheat facing a Native American holding corn, symbolize agriculture. A clock between the sculptures finishes it off.

Ceres herself, holding both wheat and corn, is molded from aluminum, designed by sculptor John Storrs. Following Art Deco principles, her body is a bit flattened, and she is without facial features. Local myth incorrectly says the statue was so high up no one would see her lack of a face. In fact, there was a rooftop observatory when the building opened. Visitors could look her in the eye from day one.

Architect Helmut Jahn's 24-story addition, done in glass and steel in 1980, faces Van Buren Street and features a 12-story atrium, creating a second, large trading floor. With changes in technology, however, no raucous trading floors are needed today; trading is done much more quietly via computers.

The building was designated a Chicago Landmark in May 1977; it was named a National Historic Landmark and entered on the National Register of Historic Places in June 1978.

Washington Street Tiffany Dome

78 East Washington Street

CHICAGO CULTURAL CENTER

(CHICAGO PUBLIC LIBRARY)

1897: Shepley, Rutan & Coolidge
2008 Tiffany dome renovation: Holabird & Root; 2021 GAR dome restoration: Harboe Architects

Opened in 1897 as the Chicago Public Library, this building was a compromise between those seeking a library and Civil War veterans wanting a memorial on the same site. The resulting Beaux Arts–style building served both. Beautiful ornamentation inside and out is highlighted by a set of exquisite Tiffany domes.

After the 1871 Great Chicago Fire, English donors sent 8,000 books to replace those lost from the city's library. Unbeknownst to them, no free public library existed before the fire; the donation spurred a new building.

The exterior is of Bedford limestone and granite. Elements of the interior, derived from the Italian Renaissance, include walls covered in wood or marble, some wainscoted (half-way up), others paneled entirely in marble. Floors are exquisite mosaics.

Off the Washington Street entrance, the grand staircase of white Carrara marble features balustrades inlaid with mosaics of marble and glass medallions of dark green Irish glass. Above the third floor's Preston Bradley Hall is the first massive stained-glass Tiffany & Co.–designed dome. It is breathtaking: 38 feet in diameter, made of 30,000 glass pieces, replicating fish scales, surrounding signs of the zodiac. Reputedly it is the largest Tiffany dome of its type in the world.

From the Randolph Street entrance, a similar staircase leads to the Grand Army of the Republic Memorial Hall and the second Tiffany dome, this one 40 feet in diameter, with 50,000 pieces of art glass.

In 1977, the building was converted to a cultural center, with free art galleries. In 2017, a mural was painted on the west exterior wall by artist Kerry James Marshall honoring 20 prominent Chicago women.

The building was named to the National Register of Historic Places in July 1972. In November 1976 it became a Chicago Landmark.

Block bounded by Dearborn Street, Jackson Boulevard, Clark and Adams Streets

CHICAGO FEDERAL CENTER

1959–1974: Ludwig Mies van der Rohe; Schmidt, Garden & Erikson; C. F. Murphy Associates; A. Epstein & Sons, associate architects

The three buildings that form the Chicago Federal Center—the Dirksen US Courthouse, 219 South Dearborn Street; the Kluczynski (Office) Building, 230 South Dearborn Street, and the US Post Office, 211 South Clark Street—together are standout icons celebrating Chicago's 20th-century love affair with Modernism.

Traditionally, US government buildings resembled Greek or Roman temples. Here, federal architecture joined the 20th century and said clearly that government buildings do not need Neo-Classical columns to have stature.

This trio is sleek, without applied ornamentation, steel and bronze-tinted glass buildings set around a plain plaza. All were set along a geometric grid. Their dark glass and steel presentation is mitigated by the bright red/vermillion Alexander Calder stabile sculpture, *Flamingo* (1974), sitting on an angle in the plaza—a study in contrast.

Despite all the architectural names above, the style is pure Miesian (also called Mid-Century Modern or International Style), architecture done by the master, Ludwig Mies van der Rohe. Mies brought the concept of Modernism to Chicago from Germany, where he had headed the Bauhaus, a school of modern design, until the 1930s, when it was shuttered by the Nazis. Coming to Chicago, Mies was appointed director of the architecture program at what would become the Illinois Institute of Technology (today, Illinois Tech). There he trained a generation of architects in Bauhaus philosophy. His dictum, "Less is more," meant buildings should stand on their own, without indication of function and without applied ornamentation.

The buildings were designed with a proportional regularity and scale, both for each individual building and the relationship between them. Almost half of the 4.5-acre site is plaza. Architectural critic Franz Schulze called the overall vision "a monumental urban presence."

The trio was added to the National Register of Historic Places in 2008.

Block bounded by Washington, Randolph, Dearborn, and Clark Streets

(RICHARD J.) DALEY CENTER

(CHICAGO CIVIC CENTER)

1965: C. F. Murphy Associates, Jacques Brownson, architect; Skidmore, Owings & Merrill; Loebl, Schlossman & Bennett

Poet Carl Sandburg called Chicago the "City of Big Shoulders." The Daley Center exemplifies that description. A great example of Mid-Century Modernism style, steel and glass without applied ornamentation, the bold, muscular building stands strong in an extraordinary public space.

The center, named for Mayor Richard J. Daley, appears monumental in its height, but welcoming via its plaza. The plaza is enhanced by, if perhaps incomprehensible to some, its statue by world-renowned sculptor Pablo Picasso. The first major public building built in Modernist rather than Neo-Classical style, the Daley Center is in striking contrast to the heavily ornamented Neo-Classical 1905 City-County Building across the street.

The 31-story structure is a grid of glass and steel, with overly long bays, up to 87 feet wide. The spandrels under the windows stretch across the facade like girders on a bridge. The highly unusual steel color comes from Cor-Ten, a steel first developed for railroad use. It rusts upon itself, changing from its original orangish to today's brown color. The glass-enclosed lobby is set back and transparent. The interior includes 120 court and hearing rooms, a law library, and office spaces, many with 12-foot-high ceilings. Twenty-six courtrooms extend up two stories.

The Picasso, titled *Untitled*, also constructed of Cor-Ten, was one of the city's first public art installations. It draws many to it, including children who use its base as a slide. Disliked or misunderstood when it was first unveiled in 1967—many at the time asked why there wasn't a statue of Ernie Banks, Chicago's favorite Cubs baseball player—it has grown into a city icon. The plaza is active through the spring and summer with farmers markets, performances, and people just seeking to enjoy an outdoor lunch.

The building was named a Chicago Landmark in November 2002.

343 South Dearborn Street

FISHER BUILDING

1896: D. H. Burnham & Co., Charles Atwood, architect
1907: Addition: Peter J. Weber

Golden in the light of western sunsets, this is a fabulous Chicago Commercial–style building that combines structure with fantasy. Technologically, it was the epitome of a modern skyscraper at the turn of the century, and then architect Charles Atwood applied Neo-Gothic ornamentation that amuses as it provides aesthetic appeal. No other similarly styled building comes anywhere near this one in its whimsy—much of it playing off the name of first owner Lucius Fisher.

This 18-story building was constructed with a steel frame, so technologically advanced that it went up quickly—reportedly about a floor a day. It is said that members of the public brought their chairs, set them up across the street (at the Monadnock Building), and watched as floors "flew" into place. It was a decided change from masonry buildings that took years to complete. The building structure is supported internally, and the walls become a decorative glass curtain wall hanging from the framework.

The building is clad in pale salmon-colored glazed terra-cotta (clay put in molds and baked at high temperatures in a kiln to make it fire resistant), which is also used for the cornice. The highly distinctive ornamentation is an abundance of Gothic tracery, molds of eagles, and fleurs-de-lis (French symbols for royalty), with frogs and salamanders thrown in for good measure. Fish—pun on Fisher—are found over the three entrances, on Dearborn, Plymouth, and Van Buren Streets. Along Van Buren, which at the time had no elevated train tracks in front so was considered the main entrance, sea nymphs riding huge fish top the arched entrance doorway, while salamanders crawl downward into the sidewalk/sea.

The building was named a Chicago Landmark in June 1978, having already been named to the National Register of Historic Places in March 1976.

400 SOUTH STATE STREET

HAROLD WASHINGTON LIBRARY CENTER

1991: Hammond, Beeby & Babka

A rollicking example of Post-Modernism, the Harold Washington Library Center anchors Chicago's south downtown, occupying an entire block. Looking down from its roofline corners are towering aluminum owls, symbolizing knowledge, and the solid red-brick, 800,000-square-foot building beneath them opens as a book bespeaking "library." The building is deeply rooted in the city—much of its ornamentation honors Chicago.

Post-Modernism, the late 1980s–1990s style that evolved after decades of non-ornamented, stark Modernist buildings, presents buildings that are contextual, reflecting their environment, often with monumentality and some whimsy. Here, architect Thomas Beeby puts the city front and center. The rough granite base on three of the building's faces references older, nearby neighbors. Medallions with the face of Ceres, the Roman goddess of grain, refer viewers to the same goddess in a statue atop the nearby Chicago Board of Trade building. Her corn necklace and the medallions at the bottom of festoons made of wheat and corn reinforce Chicago's strong connections to grain trading.

Other medallions include the so-called Windy Man—with his cheeks bulging out ready to blow—referring to Chicago's nickname, "Windy City." The triangular ornament or pediment atop the building recalls the Art Institute of Chicago's pediment, and the layered, recessed arches honor architect Louis Sullivan's Auditorium Theatre Building. The western wall is in the Modernist style, all glass.

The library is named for Chicago's first Black mayor, Harold Washington. Campaigning, he supported building a new central library, but he died in office in 1987. That is the same year the architectural competition for the library opened. Named in his honor, this is the largest open-stack library in the nation.

P.S. Despite the Windy Man image, the nickname doesn't come from Chicago's wind. It was bestowed on the city because of blowhard politicians who successfully lobbied to bring the 1893 World's Fair to Chicago.

30 West Monroe Street

INLAND STEEL BUILDING

1956–7: Skidmore, Owings & Merrill, Bruce Graham and Walter Netsch, project designers

The first tall commercial building constructed in Chicago's Loop after the Depression and World War II. The first skyscraper with flat, unadorned external supports and a glass curtain wall. The first to be built on steel pilings instead of concrete. The first building with an attached structure for service and mechanical systems. The first major high-rise with indoor parking.

A building of firsts, yes, but first and foremost a stunner of a skyscraper, with green-tinted windows juxtaposed against a shiny brushed stainless-steel frame. This is a streamlined structure, what's been called the purest example of Miesian style. Yet this Mid-Century Modernist–style building with no ornamentation was not designed by Modernist master Ludwig Mies van der Rohe, but by SOM architects Walter Netsch and Bruce Graham.

The structure that began downtown's postwar renaissance has become an icon. Its site plan is excellent, putting its best face forward to the street.

The office tower seemingly floats above its glass-enclosed, transparent lobby. Built of stainless steel, which, ironically, was not a product Inland specifically produced but an advertisement for the 20th-century steel industry, the 19-story office building exudes lightness and grace. Because the columns are on the outside, each interior floor has uninterrupted space.

The mechanicals—heating, ventilation, and air-conditioning systems together with elevators, loading docks, mail room, and garage entrance—live in the 25-story windowless tower to the east. A similar configuration could not be built today; it does not meet current building codes.

Green Solex windows were dual-glazed "environmental" glass—the green color enabled the glass to work similarly to clear glass but added infrared-absorbing qualities to alleviate excess heat from the sun.

The building was named a Chicago Landmark in October 1998; it was added to the National Register of Historic Places in February 2009.

140 South Dearborn Street

MARQUETTE BUILDING

1895: Holabird & Roche

The Marquette is a magnificent example of a Chicago Commercial–style office building, augmented by one of the most exquisite and unusual lobbies in Chicago.

The 16-story steel skeleton is covered in brick and matte-finish chocolate-brown terra-cotta. Commercial-style buildings typically feature a tripartite division: a base, a shaft of repeating floors, and on top, a cornice, a decorative projection at the roof level. Here, four high-relief bronzes over the main entrance tell the story of French missionary Père (French for father) Jacques Marquette's life, designed by Hermon A. MacNeil. Panther-head push plates adorn the revolving entrance doors.

The Marquette's windows are named for the city, their function to allow light and air into the offices. Chicago windows are traditionally in three parts: two smaller, double-hung sash windows flank a large, central fixed pane. Here, the central window is divided.

Inside, the breathtaking Carrara marble hexagonal two-story rotunda is a memorial to Marquette. Three mosaic murals by Tiffany & Co. done in glass, semi-precious gems, and mother of pearl tell the story of voyages into the Northwest Territory by Marquette, Louis Jolliet, and expeditions of voyageurs (explorers). Twenty bronze heads of either explorers or Native Americans, by sculptor Edward Kemeys, top the elevator doors on the lobby's two floors.

The lavish artwork resulted from the belief of the building's rental agent, Owen Aldis, that a well-appointed lobby lured excellent clients. Aldis, an amateur historian, translated Marquette's diaries from the French, hoping to make history easily accessible.

In 2001, building owner the John D. and Catherine T. MacArthur Foundation launched an extensive restoration; the entire structure was restored to its original beauty, inside and out.

The Marquette Building became a city landmark in 1975. It was listed on the National Register of Historic Places in 1973 and named a National Historic Landmark in 1976.

MARQUETTE
FANNIE MAY CANDIES
OPEN
OPEN
140

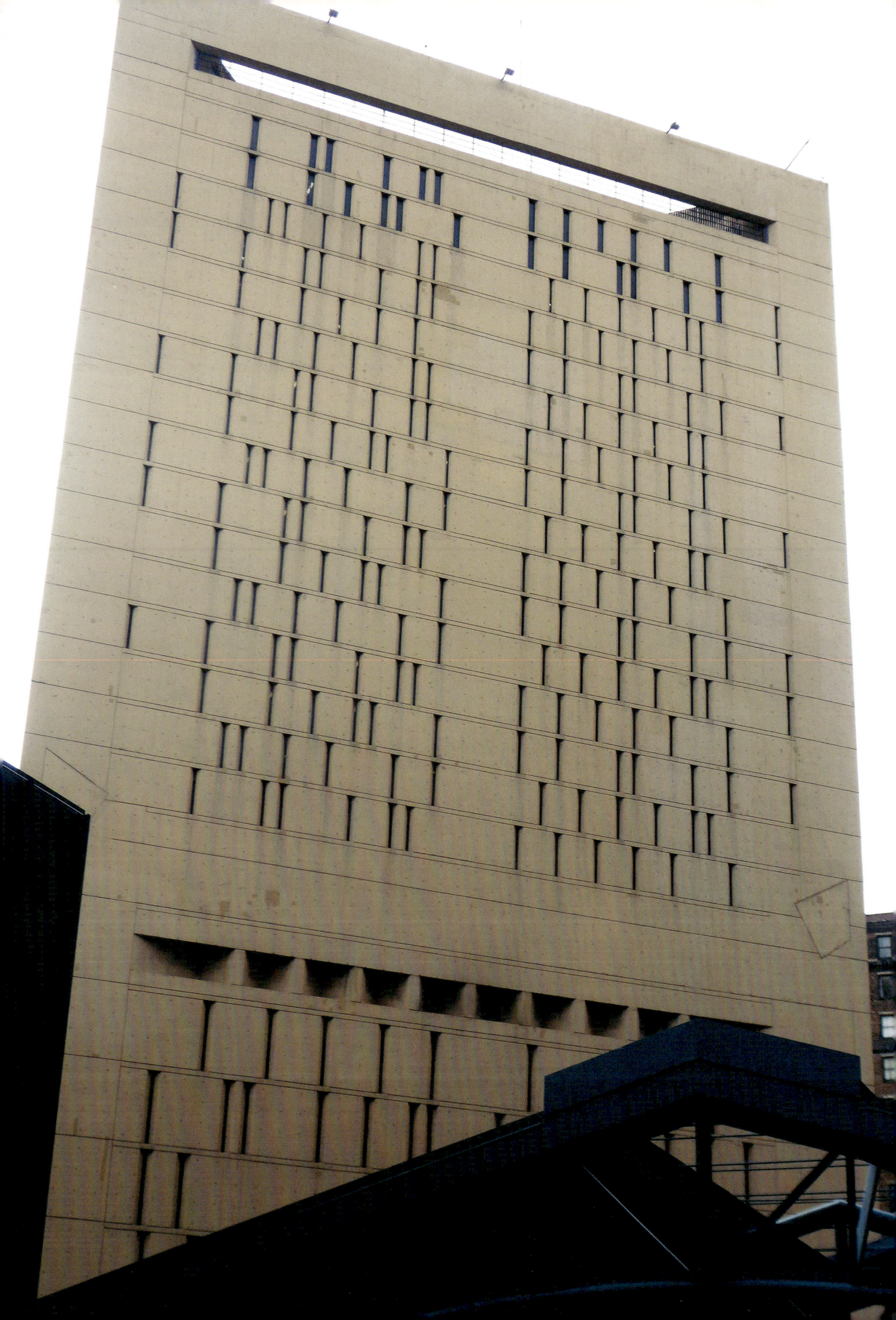

77 West
Van Buren Street

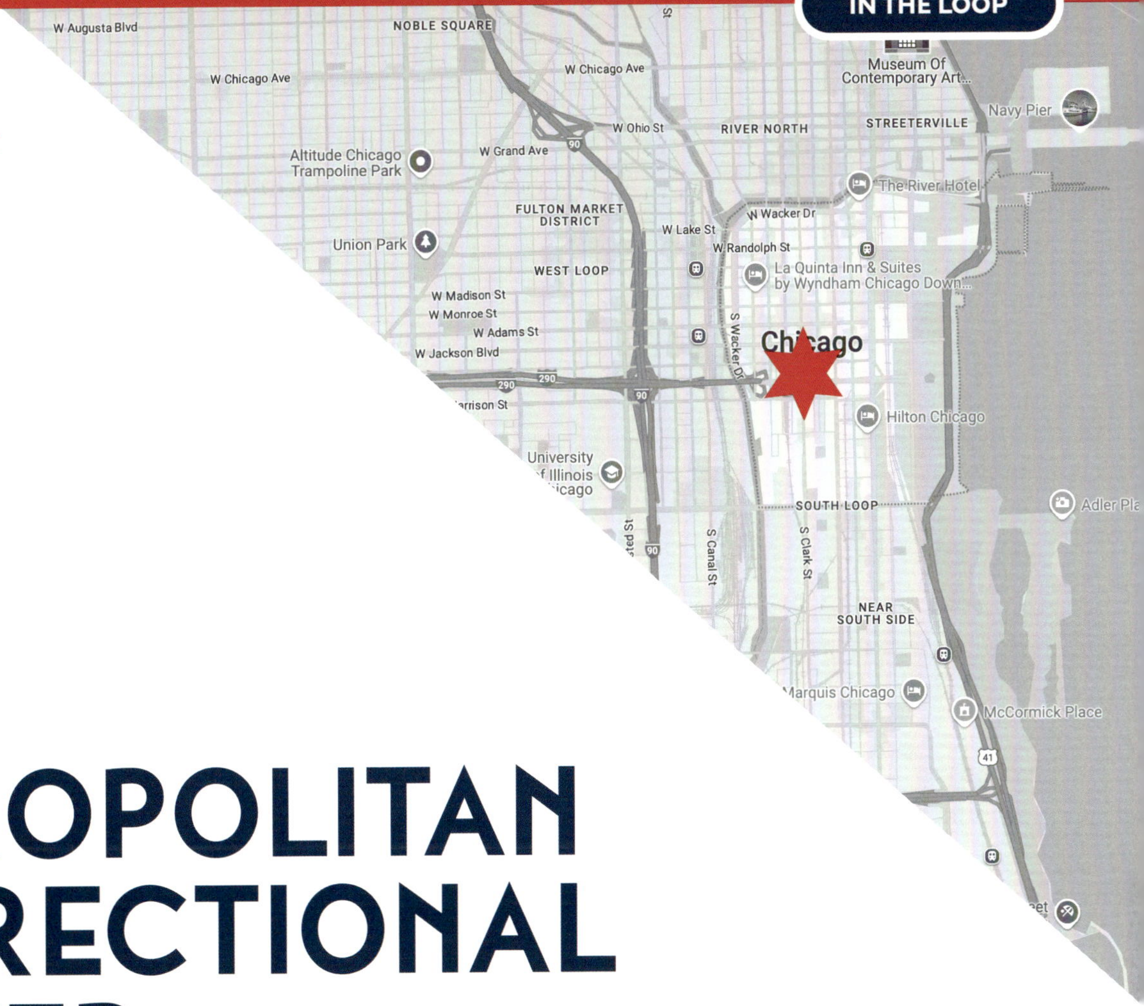

METROPOLITAN CORRECTIONAL CENTER

1975: Harry Weese and Associates

Look at it from one angle, and it appears to be flat; look at it from another and you find the triangle. If you are old enough, it may remind you of a computer punch card. However you look, you still are likely to be surprised to find that this is a jail—done in a Modernist style for sure, looking like an ordinary skyscraper, and located in the heart of downtown Chicago, but still a jail.

The Metropolitan Correctional Center, its formal name, designed by architect Harry Weese, is a holding area for those awaiting trial at the nearby Chicago Federal Center. It is a detention center run by the Federal Bureau of Prisons, one of three that were built in the 1970s with an eye toward strict but humane treatment of inmates.

The building is a right-angle triangle of reinforced concrete, 28 stories high. This is not your typical federal prison—the windows are unique. Floor-to-ceiling slits, seven feet long and a mere five inches wide on the upper floors, slightly larger on the floors below (up to 10 inches), the windows' narrowness was enough to preclude bars on cell windows. Ostensibly, the openings made the building escape-proof. In fact, twice prisoners did escape, a pair in 1985 and a second pair in 2012. All were recaptured.

The triangular layout allows for easy patrolling of the cells from the central core. Originally, the cells were made as comfortable as possible with built-in hardwood beds and desks. Most of these features have been removed. At the top of the building is an outdoor recreational area, and inmates are often seen by—and wave to—tourists in the area.

Unless the inmates are out, however, it is easy to forget the purpose of the building and instead just admire its sleek, interesting look.

53 West Jackson Boulevard

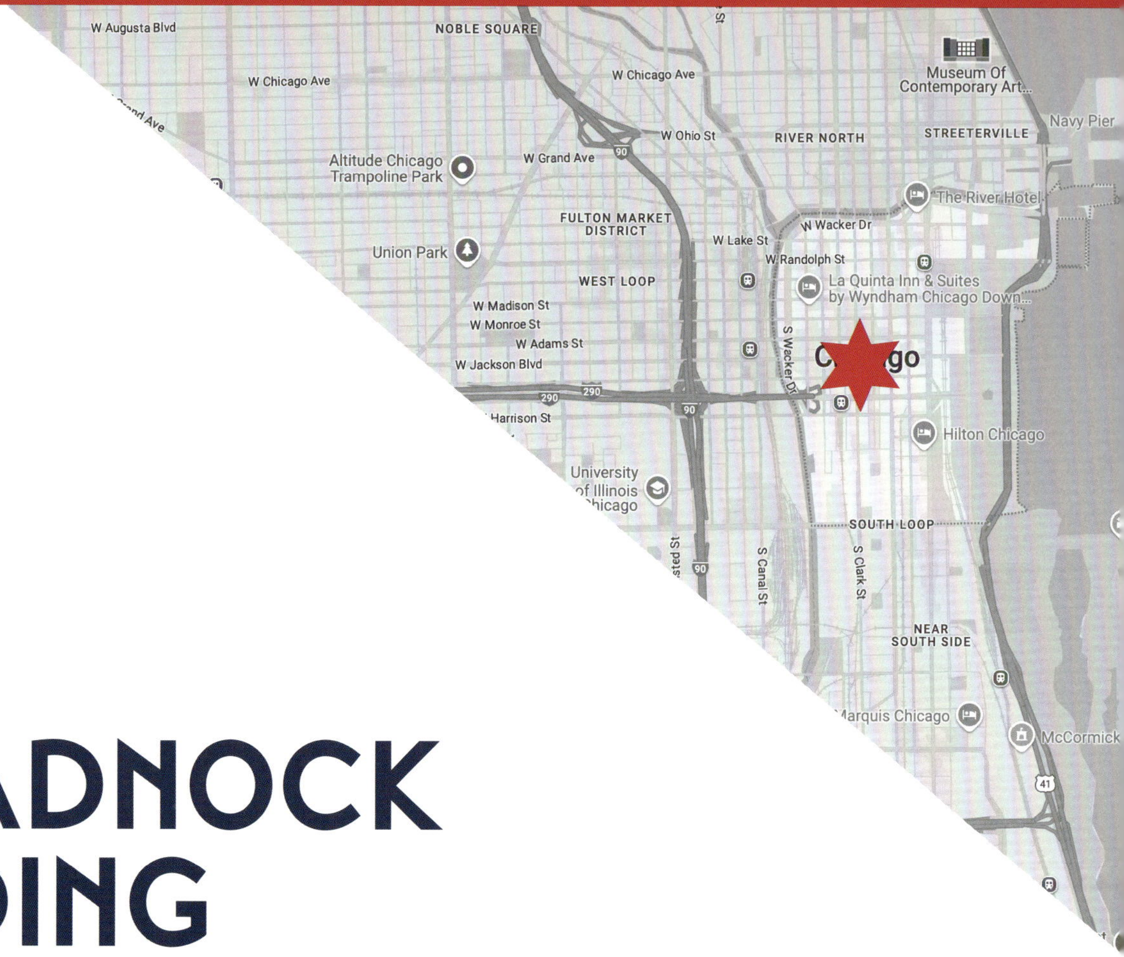

MONADNOCK BUILDING

1891: North side: Burnham & Root; 1893: South side: Holabird & Roche

It rises like the mountain range for which it was named: 16 stories high with massively thick walls. When built, the Monadnock was the world's tallest office building; today, it is one of the world's highest masonry load-bearing buildings.

The masonry, or brick-on-brick, construction of the northern half compares to the south's steel framing, which uses vertical steel in the outer walls. Attention focuses on the north's granite entrances, six-foot-thick corner piers, and brick cladding. No ornamentation is needed; the structure provides the design, with an inward curve at the second story, window bays on each level upward, and a curve back out at the 14th floor, somewhat suggestive of Egyptian architecture. The south end's window patterns, terra-cotta cladding, and doorway ornamentation speak differently—toward what will become typical skyscraper construction.

Because of its narrow lot, light is brought inside through the outer bay windows. Interior corridors are partially lit from stairwell skylights. The interesting lobby is dark, featuring marble mosaic floors and the first structural use of aluminum stairways. Retail shops line the lower floor; offices are above. The upper-level corridors flash with golden oak trim, marble wainscoting, uniquely designed hardware (doorknobs, hinges), chipped-glass partitions, and mosaic floors, which have been lovingly restored.

The building uses architect John Wellborn Root's invention of a series of floating rafts (grillage) to stabilize its heavy foundation.

The Monadnock bespeaks architectural transition, from the end of masonry construction to the future of steel frame skyscrapers—lighter, less costly, and easier to soar to greater heights.

Called a Chicago "Architectural Landmark" as far back as 1958, the Monadnock was listed on the National Register of Historic Places in November 1970. It became an official Chicago Landmark in November 1973 and is included in the 1976 National Historic Landmark Printing House Row North Historic District.

MONADNOCK
OPTIMO
51
55

BACH
MOZART
SCHUBERT
THEODORE THOMAS
ORCHESTRA HALL
220

220 South Michigan Avenue

ORCHESTRA HALL AT SYMPHONY CENTER

1905: D. H. Burnham & Co.

Chicago has long fought to be a cultural center as well as an industrial city. The Chicago Orchestra was founded in 1891, headed by famous conductor Theodore Thomas, who was brought from New York to be maestro for the new group, which initially played in the more-than-4,000-seat Auditorium Theatre. But very quickly Thomas desired his own hall. He needed fewer seats to profitably run subscription concerts, and he wanted a more intimate space, one he did not have to share with ballet or opera companies.

In the space of one year, Thomas raised $750,000. Architect Daniel Burnham, himself an amateur musician and on the orchestra's board of directors, created the plans for this gem of a hall, seating 2,522.

The building, which opened in 1905, reflects Burnham's interest in revival styles—using ideas from history. This Neo-Georgian, modeled after English architecture during the era of Georgian kings, features a dark-pink brick with white limestone facade. Burnham created a homey rather than pompous look, accessible not aloof. Three arched windows are capped with Georgian fan lights. On either side are rectangular double-casement windows capped by triangular pediments.

Above the entryway are the names of five great composers: Bach, Mozart, Beethoven, Schubert, and Wagner. Brahms, often grouped with the great composers, was considered to be too modern in 1905 to be included.

The ensemble was formally named the Chicago Symphony Orchestra in 1913. Building on its own success, in 1993, the CSO embarked on a $120 million addition and renovation designed by Skidmore, Owings & Merrill that incorporated the building next door into what is today the Symphony Center campus.

Orchestra Hall was designated a National Historic Landmark in April 1994. It was listed on the National Register of Historic Places in 1978 and has been included in the Chicago Landmark Historic Michigan Boulevard District since February 2002.

230 North Michigan Avenue

PENDRY HOTEL

(CARBIDE AND CARBON BUILDING)

1929: Burnham Brothers

It gleams in the sun, popping its cork on the Chicago skyline, a dark-green building trimmed in gold, akin to a champagne bottle.

In the mid-1920s, the Union Carbide and Carbon Co., makers of dry cell batteries, wanted a spectacular regional headquarters. They commissioned the Burnham Brothers, Hubert and Daniel Jr., to design it.

The resulting 37-story steel frame skyscraper was clad with fire-resistant terra-cotta in a distinctive green that highlighted the gold- and bronze-colored terra-cotta ornamentation. At the top of the shaft, the gold becomes real, 24-karat in the thinnest of sheets, one-5,000th of an inch.

Built in Chicago's so-called Golden Age, 1890s–1930s, the building is an impressive example of Art Deco, the Jazz Age's preferred style, with designs that eliminate horizontal impediments, allowing eyes easily to soar upward. The scrolling bronze grillwork on the first few exterior polished granite floors and the sumptuous interior of this Michigan Avenue skyscraper create a visual stunner.

Its tower is set back from the street, a response to Chicago's 1923 zoning law, which sought to allow air and light to reach the street.

Whether the building was truly meant to mimic a champagne bottle is unclear; some call it an urban myth. But others point to Burnham family memoirs that seem to corroborate the story. No matter. It still pops.

Named a Chicago Landmark in 1996, it was listed on the National Register of Historic Places' Historic Michigan Avenue Heritage District in November 1978. The building was converted to a hotel in 2004, opening with the Hard Rock Hotel until 2017. The next year the St. Jane, named in honor of Chicago's social worker and reformer Jane Addams, opened, closing in 2020. Pendry Hotel occupies the building today.

610 SOUTH MICHIGAN AVENUE

SPERTUS INSTITUTE FOR JEWISH LEARNING AND LEADERSHIP

2007: Krueck Sexton Partners

"Light" is the word best used to describe the Spertus Institute. With more than 726 pieces of glass in 556 different shapes forming the building facade, natural light penetrates a windowless interior, providing incredible views. The fractured glass shapes refract and reflect visions of Grant Park's trees, landscape, and sky.

A second word is "complementary," as this is a Post-Modernist building that fits in or complements the buildings around it in the landmarked 2002 Historic Michigan Boulevard District. Often called the Michigan Avenue Streetwall, it is a stretch of buildings along Michigan Avenue from Randolph Street (150 North) to Roosevelt Road (1200 South) from the architectural period following the 1871 Great Chicago Fire through the 1920s. Spertus was built on what was an empty spot on the streetwall, and rather than fight the location, its architects integrated the building into the streetscape, both its height and size, and in the process designed an architecturally significant building.

The Spertus Institute began in 1924 as the College of Jewish Studies. In 1942, it was state licensed to grant degrees. The school moved into its first building in 1946; from the 1940s to '60s it served as the primary Midwest institution for Jewish education. In 1968, Maurice Spertus donated an expansive collection of Jewish ceremonial objects, launching the Spertus Museum. In 1970, the school changed its name to Spertus College of Judaica honoring both Maurice and his brother Herman. In 1993, the institution became the Spertus Institute of Jewish Studies.

The building's "light" symbolism is reflected in Spertus's logo, a flame with the Hebrew words *yehi*, or "be the light." The building houses classrooms, offices, a library, a 400-seat theater/auditorium, and a variety of event spaces. In January 2013, the name was changed to Spertus Institute for Jewish Learning and Leadership.

1 West Washington Street; 32 North State Street

STAYPINEAPPLE HOTEL

(RELIANCE BUILDING)

1895: Burnham & Root; D. H. Burnham and Co., John W. Root, Charles Atwood
1996: Exterior renovation: McClier; 1999: Adaptive reuse: Antunovich Associates; McClier, restoration architects

This stunning glass-and-white terra-cotta building has been dubbed "proto-Modernist," meaning it doesn't reflect its heavily ornamented, stone-clad Gilded Age contemporaries. Rather, it portends what will be arriving with post-World War II Modernism—glass, lots of glass. The large plate windows that foreshadow the 20th century cover about 70 percent of the 19th-century building.

Its projecting bay windows and terra-cotta cladding create the effect of lightness, thought necessary for a building designed for doctors and dentists. That cladding also was thought to be self-cleaning with rainfall, a salvation in an age when coal soot covered the city's buildings. In practice, the idea didn't work.

The building's history is a bit odd, as the granite-clad first floor and basement were designed in 1890 by John Root, yet the rest of the building was designed by Charles Atwood in 1895, following Root's death. When the building was to be built, investor and elevator entrepreneur William Hale could not get tenants on the upper floors in the existing building to give up their leases. Working around this, the contractor jacked up the upper floors, demolished the basement and first floor, and began work with the tenants in situ above. It was not until their leases ran out that Atwood, hired as Root's replacement, could finish the work on the upper floors.

The office building fell into disrepair as far back as the 1940s and was adaptively reused as a hotel in the late 1990s. Currently, it is home to the 122-room Staypineapple Hotel.

The Reliance Building was listed on the National Register of Historic Places in 1970; in 1976, it was designated a National Historic Landmark and is part of the Loop Retail Historic District. It became a Chicago Landmark in 1995.

NORDSTROM rack

1 South State Street

SULLIVAN CENTER

(ORIGINALLY SCHLESINGER & MAYER CO.; CARSON PIRIE SCOTT & CO.)

1899, 1904: Louis H. Sullivan
1906: Addition: D. H. Burnham & Co.; 1961: State Street Addition: Holabird & Root

A monument to beauty through intricate designs in the cast-iron facade. A blueprint for the creation of retail spaces. The Sullivan Center is a smashing example of how architect Louis Sullivan combined exquisite ornament with the practicality of his motto: Form follows function.

"Sullivan's greatest masterpiece" and "one of the finest examples of commercial architecture in the world," says the Chicago Landmarks Commission report. The building is a steel skeletal construction with fireproofing, which became the basis for future steel-frame, high-rise construction. It opened into expansive, airy interiors, great for sales floors, so subsequently also was the model for future department store construction.

But the signature feature is Sullivan's organic ornament, design inspired by native Midwestern prairie plants. The lower floors are sheathed in dark-green cast-iron enhanced by elaborate patterns: leaves, berries, flowers, vines, and geometric forms. The corner entrance rotunda is emphasized with additional ornament, with Sullivan's initials woven in above the corner entry. The building was and is today crowned by a decorative overhanging cornice.

The original store consisted of the first three (window) bays along Madison Street, setting the model for the addition, which was expanded after Carson purchased it in 1904. That brought five additional bays, additional height topped with the cornice, and the magnificent rounded entry on the corner of Madison and State Streets, the center of Chicago's street grid.

Major 21st-century restoration included replacing the long-lost cornice and conversion to a mixed-used building with retail, offices, and galleries.

Named a Chicago Landmark in November 1970, the building was placed on the National Register of Historic Places in April 1970 and designated a National Historic Landmark five years later.

209 South LaSalle Street

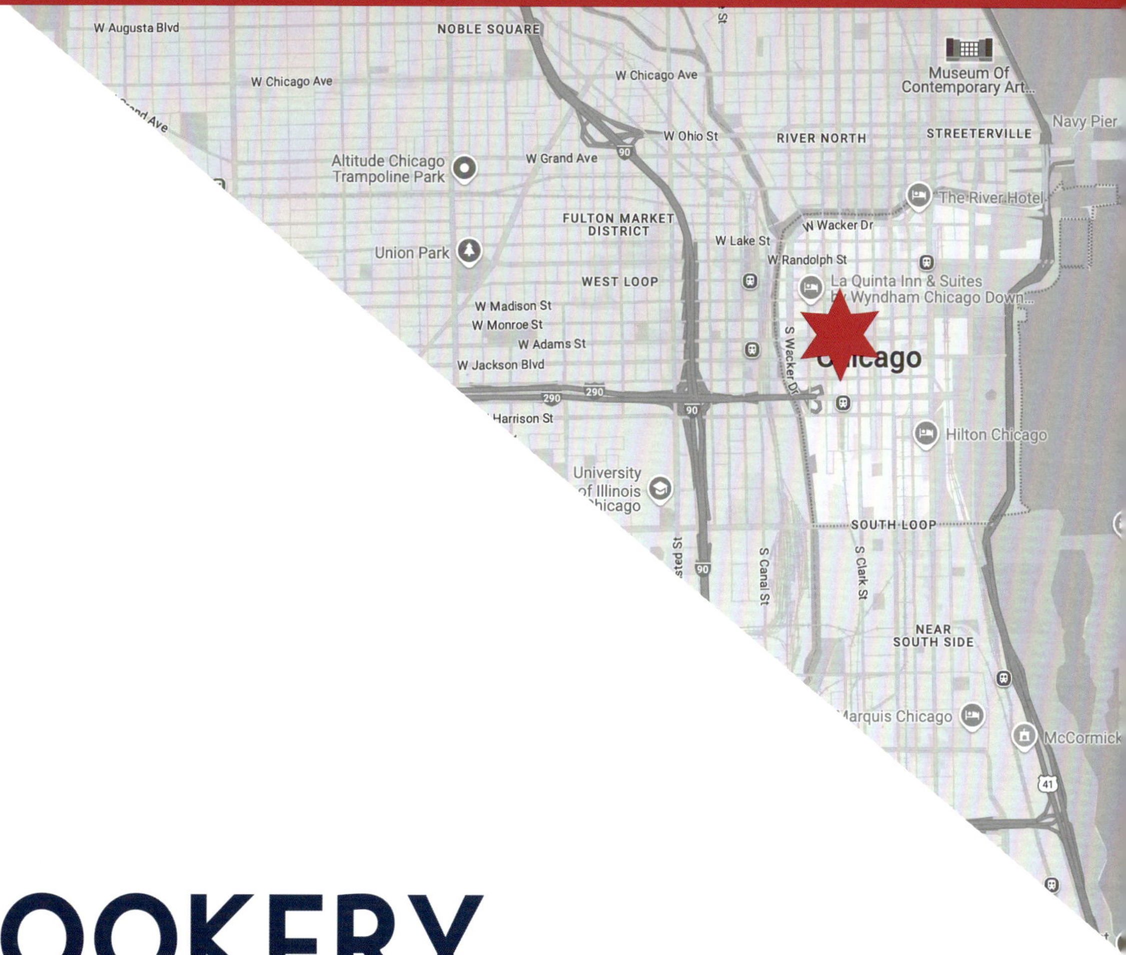

THE ROOKERY

1888: Burnham & Root

Built on the site of a former city hall water tower that attracted birds, the whimsically named Rookery is a transitional building created from both traditional masonry load-bearing materials and what would later become the norm for skyscrapers, metal framing. The building's moniker may be in jest, but its exterior is impressive and its interior atrium spectacular, a Frank Lloyd Wright creation that is both delicate and graceful.

On its north and west sides the building is held up with masonry—bricks and stone—but facing south and east along Quincy Court, beginning at the third floor, a metal frame rising upward supports the weight of the building, the innovative technology for the time.

The Rookery, the oldest standing skyscraper in Chicago, is an 11-story building with a two-story, rusticated (unpolished) granite base, including large arched entryways adorned in terra-cotta ornament, mostly portraits of birds. The building rises in red-brown brick adding bay windows, turrets beginning at the eighth floor, and then granite columns—drawing your eyes ever upward. Architect John Wellborn Root integrated numerous shapes, textures, and materials on the facades with interconnected designs.

Inside is the magnificent, soaring two-story atrium and light court that floods the interior and its retail shops and offices with natural light. In 1992, the interior was restored to the 1905 Wright design, with its walls and staircases in white marble incised with gold featuring Wrightian-style planters on the stairway pedestals.

Elevators, added to the lobby in the 1930s renovation, feature Art Deco–designed birds "flying" on their golden entry doors. This spectacular setting is often used for weddings and gala events.

Named a Chicago Landmark in July 1972, the Rookery was placed on the National Register of Historic Places even earlier, in April 1970, and named a National Historic Landmark in May 1975.

CLARK
Prime | Capri Interests
Google

100 West Randolph Street

THOMPSON CENTER

(STATE OF ILLINOIS BUILDING)

1984: Helmut Jahn

When it opened it looked like an alien spaceship. But for those who appreciate Post-Modernism, it was a gem. Now under scaffolding, the building is being converted to the new Google Center or Googleplex Chicago—we do not yet have a moniker for the building with its new function.

Originally, it was the State of Illinois Building, home to the state government offices in Chicago. In 1993 it was renamed in honor of former governor James R. Thompson.

Using the same materials as Modernists—concrete, glass, and steel—Post-Modernists reconfigured straight lines and added historical references. Here, elements of a traditional 19th-century capitol building—rotunda and dome—are displayed differently. The building features a cylindrical atrium (the rotunda) going up 17 stories. The sliced-off top provides just a suggestion of a dome.

The soaring interior atrium is both colorful and whimsical, also traits of Post-Modernism. Its openness and transparency symbolize goals for government; this was emphasized with, at least initially, no office doors.

Variations of governmental red, white, and blue—here more salmon, white, and teal-blue—were jarring to many. But everyone appreciated the interior marble inlay floors on the lower level, both a food court and an entrance to a Chicago Transit Authority transit station. The CTA station will be incorporated into the repurposed building.

In 2022, the State of Illinois sold the building to Google, Inc., with a lease to allow the state to populate some offices in the restored building. The building's exterior glass was removed in the first stage of a $280 million renovation, due to be completed in 2026. Google is touting its redesign as an update that pays homage to the building's original design. That would be great.

190 South LaSalle Street

US BANK BUILDING

(190 SOUTH LASALLE STREET)

1987: John Burgee Architects with Philip Johnson; Shaw and Associates, associate architects

This Post-Modern 42-story building, the only building in Chicago designed by New York "starchitect" Philip Johnson, was inspired by historic buildings placed in the context of modern Chicago.

It has been described as being done in an "in your face" Post-Modern style. Post-Modernism was a break from the unornamented and geometric lines of the 1950s–1980s Mid-Century Modernism. The 1980s and '90s Post-Modernism espoused a more fanciful look, sometimes referencing history, with contextualized designs, meaning ones that fit well into the area, often complementing existing buildings.

Johnson, who early in his career was a "king" of Modernism, pivots here to Post-Modernism. With a building base clad in Alicante (Red Imperial) granite and shafts in Spanish Pink granite, the building features monumental 45-foot bronze-framed arched doors at the base and a two-story, steeply gabled, mint-green roof. Gables, an angled roof form belonging to earlier times, top it all off.

The gables referenced a long-demolished Daniel Burnham and John Wellborn Root–designed Masonic Temple that had stood nearby. The reddish-brown granite blocks reference its still-standing neighbor, the Rookery (1886), across the street, also designed by Burnham and Root.

On the ground level, the interior lobbies on both LaSalle and Adams Streets are monumental in height. Those on LaSalle Street focus on a vaulted ceiling of gold leaf. White marble walls, red marble columns topped with gold hand-carved capitals, and tiled floors emphasize the luxury of the building, which originally also had a law library on its top floor.

At the north end of the lobby is a huge abstract sculpture by British sculptor Anthony Caro titled Chicago Fugue, using musical instruments for its structure. On the south end, a semicircular brass-and-marble amphitheater by Norman Kelly uses real-time data inputs, like weather and time of day, to compose an ever-changing sonic environment.

SMALL Cheval

150 North Riverside Plaza

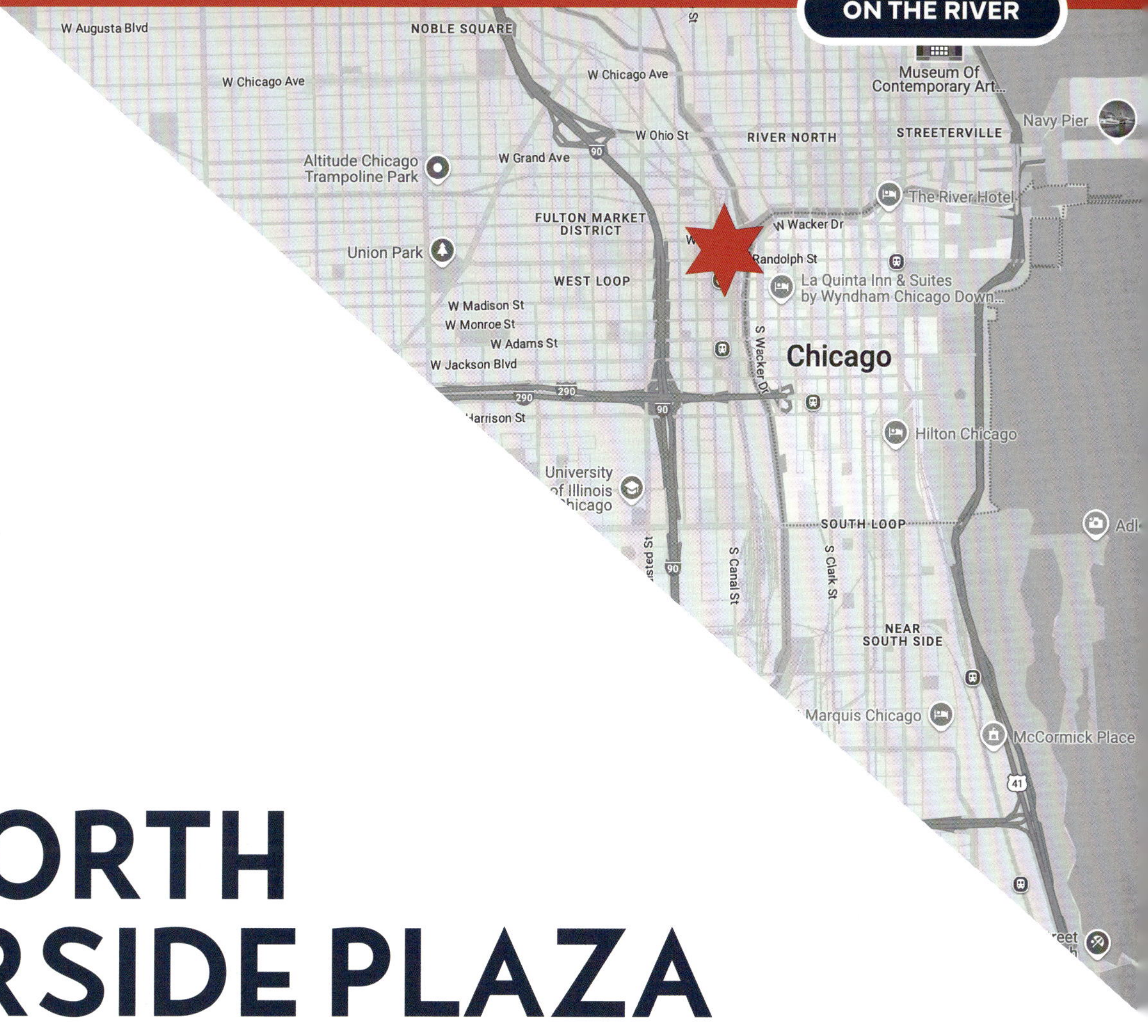

150 NORTH RIVERSIDE PLAZA

2017: Goettsch Partners

A martini glass? A tuning fork? A muscular dancer en pointe? Many nicknames exist for this beautifully thin skyscraper rising 54 stories above the Chicago River Confluence (the meeting of the river's three branches). It is a fabulous example of a Contemporary-style, super-tall building incorporating many of architecture's newest technologies.

For over 100 years the site had been considered difficult and unbuildable because the land is hemmed in by the river on one side and railroad tracks underneath. And yet, today we have a 1.2-million-square-foot office and retail building located on this 85-foot-wide area. The secret was the use of "triangular trusses." Beneath the eighth floor, massive steel columns slope inward, transferring the building's load to the central core. The columns are the largest rolled shapes in the world, made from steel that is 40 percent stronger than conventional steel. Fabricated in Luxembourg, this is its first North American use.

The concrete core has the highest-rated strength of any in the city today. And the top floor houses one of the first uses in Chicago of a tuned liquid damper system—water sloshing in 12 concrete "bathtub" tanks offsets the power of the wind.

The east side of the building is held up above an active riverwalk. The tapered underside west of the tower is enclosed in walls of highly transparent glass and houses a park.

The building's lower level, 75 percent of the lot, landscaped by Wolff Landscape Architecture, wraps around the south side of the tower, ending on the west atop a parking garage. It and the lobby entrance are off of Randolph Street.

But don't just look at the outside—come indoors to view the impressive 90-foot-high glass-enclosed lobby with a 150-foot-long multimedia wall featuring the work of local and international digital artists.

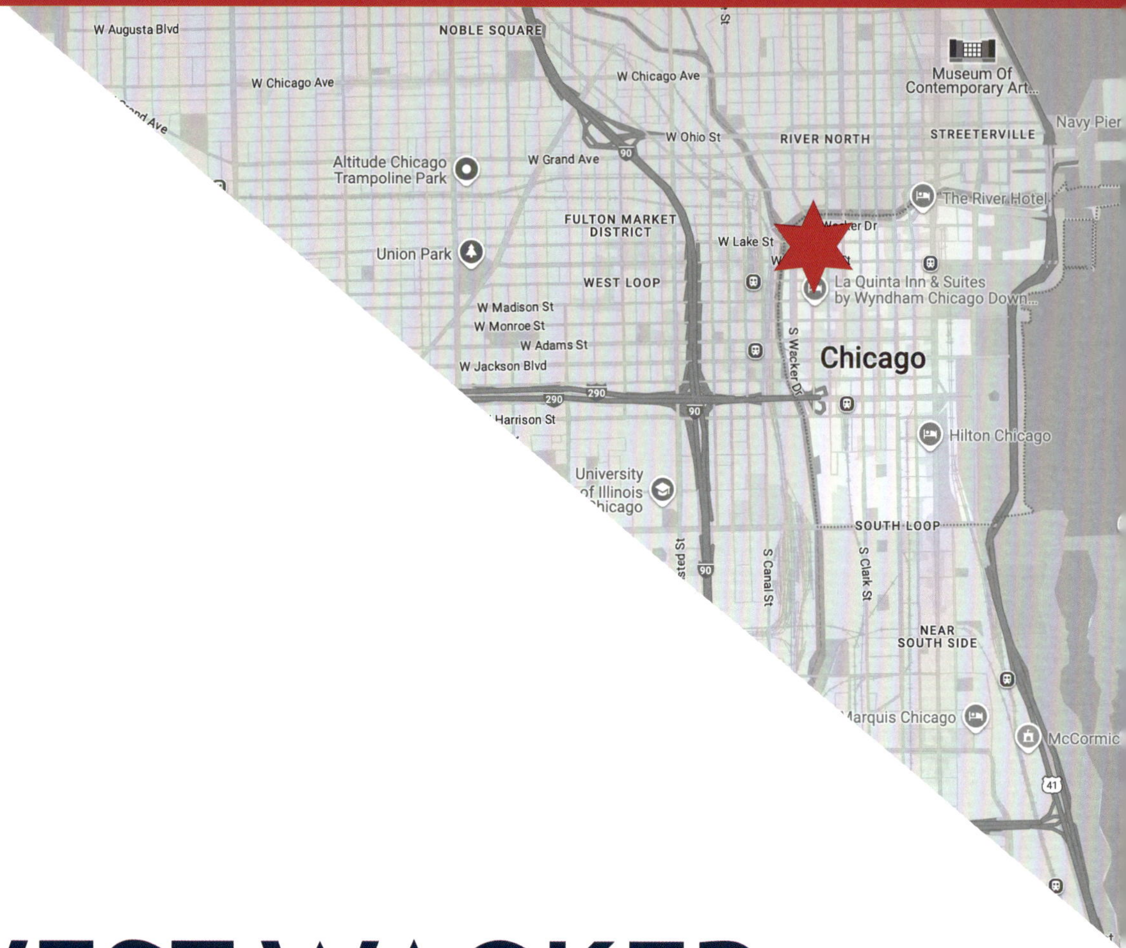

333 WEST WACKER

(NUVEEN BUILDING)

1983: KPF (formerly Kohn Pedersen Fox); Perkins & Will, associate architects

This once was hands-down the most beautiful building on the Chicago River, with its magnificent sweep along the curve of the Confluence, where the North and South Branches meet the river's Main Stem. But even with additional new competing beauties, this one still stands out. The curve of green-tinted glass echoes the color of the river, and the lovely reflection of the surrounding vistas changes depending on how the light plays on the building's face.

While some call it the city's first Post-Modern building, architect William Pedersen has been quoted as saying the building is actually "contextual." Yes, it is Post-Modern because it breaks the mold of the strongly rectangular Mid-Century Modernist steel and glass boxes. But, yes, it is also contextual, another feature of Post-Modernism, because of how it fits snugly along the river's bend and blends with its surroundings.

The design of 333 West Wacker influenced subsequent architecture along the river. KPF's appreciation for the setting and the river played a major role in following work, which took into account site placement.

The base of the building is black and gray granite to help absorb the sounds of the elevated train running along its south side. Offices begin above the level of the "L." Acoustic, sound-deafening glass was not available in 1983, but thermal windows complete the shafts of curved glass. That glass hides the supporting steel cross-bracing.

The sides that face away from the river feature porthole windows at the base, in yet another nod to the building's site. This 36-story building was the first of a series of KPF designs along the river, including 225 West Wacker and 191 North Wacker Drive.

333
West

330 NORTH WABASH AVENUE

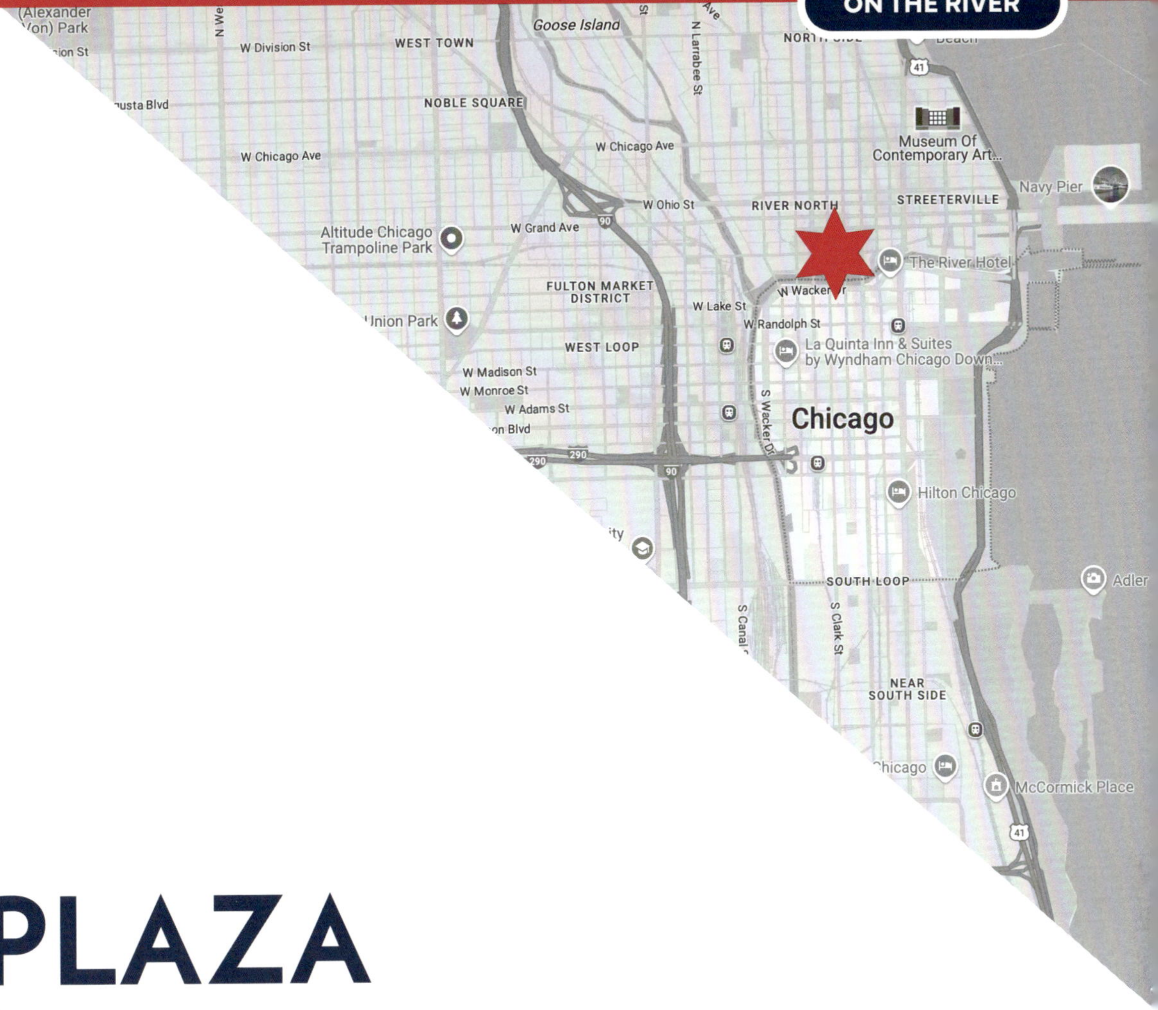

AMA PLAZA

(IBM BUILDING)

1971: Office of Mies van der Rohe; C. F. Murphy Associates, associate architects

Ludwig Mies van der Rohe was a powerhouse architect and educator in Chicago architectural history. This, his last design, is an icon, an exemplar of his Modernist philosophy.

Mies left Germany in the 1930s when the Nazis forcibly closed the Bauhaus, the German school of art and design that through the 1920s and '30s espoused a new design philosophy of sleek lines, little applied ornamentation, and the use of readily available materials.

From the dark bronze metal exterior, the building exemplifies both Mies's theory of "Less Is More" and his attention to detail. The 52-story building is on a rectangular grid, despite being on an irregular site. It is placed as far to the north end of the lot as possible, creating a plaza next to the Chicago River. As is typical with Modernist designs, the building is placed on columns, called pilotis, that lift the building above a recessed, glass-enclosed lobby.

The building was built for IBM—both its employees and a great deal of computer equipment. Mies and former student Bruno Conterato used double-glazed windows, with a thermal break between the interior and exterior. That allowed IBM to recycle the heat given off by the machines, people, and light bulbs. While it meant IBM was Chicago's most expensive office building at the time, during the 1973 oil embargo the building used 43 percent less energy than the average structure.

In February 2008 the building was designated a Chicago Landmark, 14 years before the usual 50-year requirement. It was added to the National Register of Historic Places in 2010. Today, it is home to the Langham Hotel—named in 2017 by US News and World Report as the US's best hotel and among the world's best by *Travel + Leisure*—and headquarters of the American Medical Association.

401 North Michigan Avenue

APPLE MICHIGAN AVENUE STORE

2017: Foster + Partners

A triumph of 21st-century technology, the Apple Store is truly a glass house—glass provides all the walls. Cascading down to the Chicago River, with granite stairs that run both inside and out, the walls are topped with a fiberglass roof that to many looks like the top of a MacBook laptop, although designers deny that was the intention.

The sales floor is on the Riverwalk level, and customers descend down the interior steps that are extensions of the exterior stairs; boundaries between inside and out vanish. The stairs pull customers from the Michigan Avenue–level Pioneer Court down to the riverwalk, filled with strolling tourists and locals, and providing up-close views of the traffic on the Chicago River.

The glass walls, some as tall as 32 feet, are created of panels of four one-half-inch-thick, low-iron glass layers laminated together, created by Sedak, a German glass manufacturer. The carbon-fiber composite roof is, at its thickest point, only three feet, four inches. It is supported primarily by four interior columns, which also hold the roof drains.

The building sits below Pioneer Court Plaza, named in honor of Chicago's first non–Native American settler, Jean Baptiste Point du Sable, who settled on the site in the late 18th century. He and his Potawatomi wife, Kitihawa, set up a trading post, beginning Chicago's position as trading center for the nation. Du Sable is considered the founder of Chicago, and the adjacent Michigan Avenue bridge has been named in his honor.

Apple wanted a store that would be a community gathering place. The staircases, with landings inside and out, function as a town hall space, where people can sit, talk, and watch the world go by. It is, according to Apple's chief designer, ". . . about removing boundaries between inside and outside, (and) reviving important urban connections within the city."

20 NORTH WACKER DRIVE

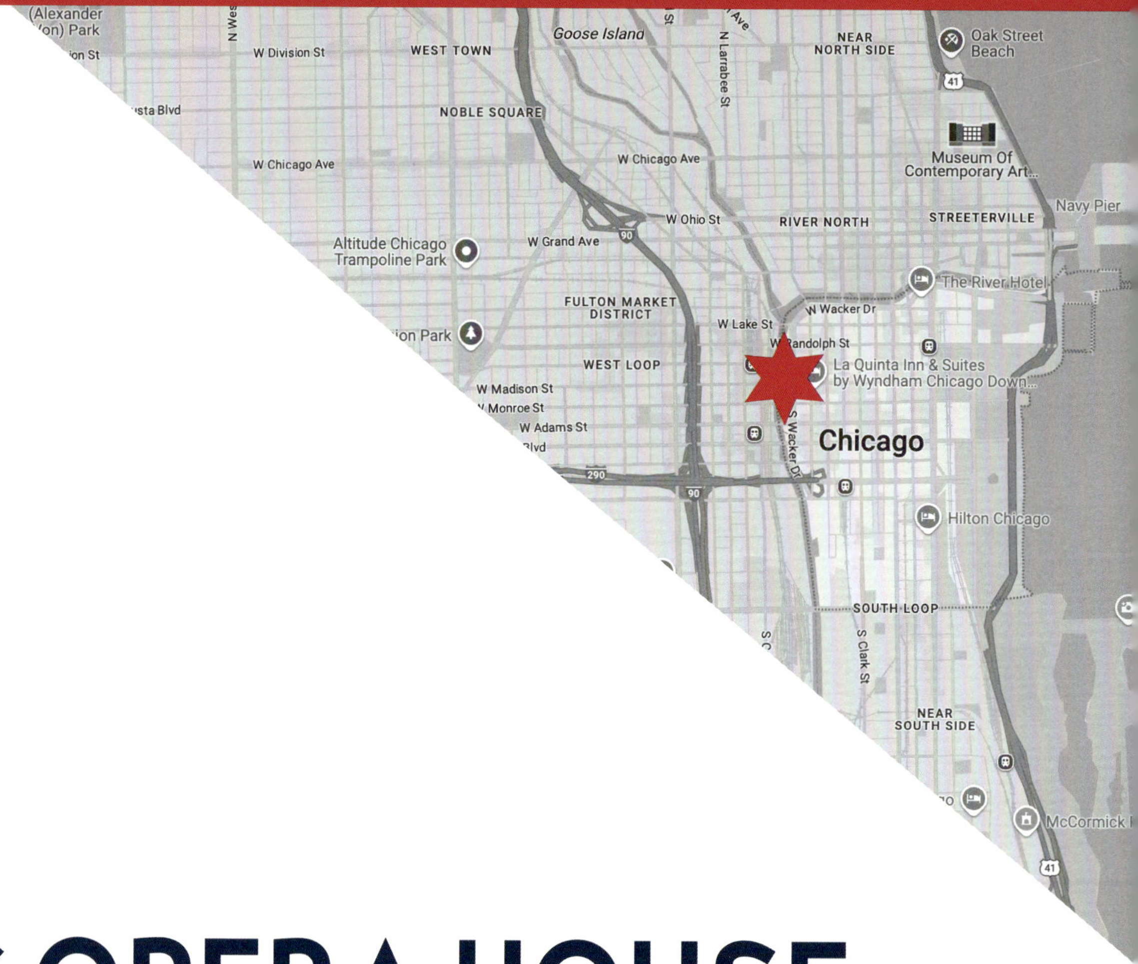

CIVIC OPERA HOUSE

1929: Graham, Anderson, Probst & White

It's a huge building, but, after all, it holds the second-largest opera stage in the US (after the Metropolitan Opera in New York). Yet, that is only part of what makes this building special; it has on its east facade a grand colonnade similar to those found in Paris's opera house. The French Neo-Classical style was chosen by architect Alfred Shaw because he thought it would "offer a sympathetic background for the old, conservative traditions of opera."

While the limestone structure and its arcade were influenced by the French, the interior features a gloriously, richly decorated Art Deco treasure. The 40-foot-high lobby space overawes, and the stage fire curtain, designed by Jules Guérin, is a dream in gold. The house seats 3,500.

The opera house was founded by Samuel Insull, a mogul who made his money in electrical and gas utilities and transportation. At one time Insull's wide-ranging business interests included ownership of the entire Chicago "L" system. Insull was looking for an opera house to replace the existing Auditorium Theatre. Hedging his bets, he added two huge wings of office space, using the rentals to partially subsidize the opera company. That makes the building look like an armchair: The 12-story opera house is the "seat," the 22-story office buildings the "arms," and a 45-story office tower the "back." Critics at the time referred to the building as "Insull's throne."

The Depression's opening stock market crash came just six days after the Civic Opera Company opened its first season with Verdi's *Aida*. That company quickly went out of business. Today, the Lyric Opera Co. owns the building. In 1993, the Civic Theatre, originally on the north end, was removed to give Lyric expanded rehearsal and storage space.

The building was named a Chicago Landmark in February 1998.

THE CIVIC OPERA HOVSE
LYRIC OPERA
OF CHICAGO
Lyric
OPERA OF
CHICAGO

505 North DuSable Lake Shore Drive

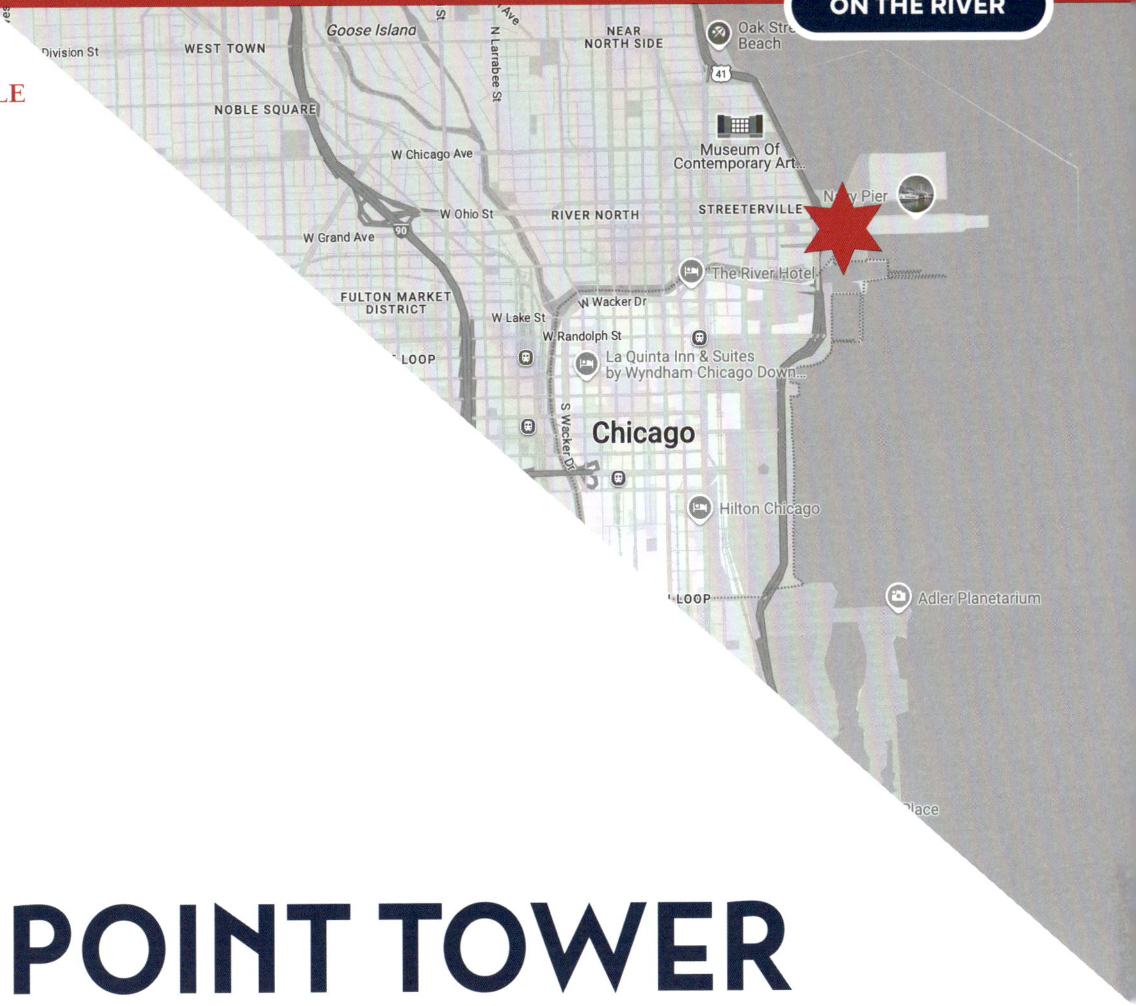

LAKE POINT TOWER

1968: Schipporeit & Heinrich

Standing alone on a site immediately east of DuSable Lake Shore Drive, on the Chicago River, Lake Point Tower appears as a giant three-leaf clover.

When it was built, it was the tallest reinforced concrete building in Chicago. It was also the tallest all-residential high-rise in the world until 1993, when Hong Kong boasted an even higher one. Here, though, it is not just the height but the curvature that gives the building its fascinating silhouette.

While the building resembles a traditional Modernist building of glass and metal, Lake Point Tower diverges from that by both the choice of materials and the use of the curve, or a three-wing construction, which adds to privacy. No unit faces into another; all the views are out to the lake or the skyline.

Extra-strength concrete is used on the lower floors, and the metal above is anodized aluminum (aluminum coated to protect against corrosion). Because of its height and location, the skyscraper was designed to withstand high winds. At its center, the triangular core, 59 feet wide, contains elevators and stairwells. This core holds the vertical weight of the building, allowing the facade's perimeter columns to be smaller.

A private 2.5-acre landscape garden and pond designed by famous landscape architect Alfred Caldwell is above the building's brick base. Below there are meeting rooms, a garage, a lobby, and a fitness center.

Lake Point Tower's location was controversial. The powers-that-be and city planners wanted to keep the lakefront as public open space. Yet, there were some sites along the river that had been kept open to erect harbor improvements. Lake Point Tower was built on a promontory of the exempted land, which was possible at the time it was built. The city afterward quickly closed the area to construction. So, now, Lake Point Tower stands in solitary beauty.

85 East Upper Wacker Drive

LONDON HOUSE HOTEL

(LONDON GUARANTEE & ACCIDENT BUILDING)

1923: Alfred S. Alschuler

Known for its smashing 360-degree skyline views from its tri-level rooftop, this 1920s skyscraper, designed by Alfred Alschuler for a British insurance company, is today a hotel. The rooftop plaza with the rounded dome, called a cupola, is a favorite photo location for Chicago brides as well as tourists.

The white, terra-cotta 22-story building stands on a corner of East Wacker Drive and Michigan Avenue, the site of Fort Dearborn, which was the US's farthest west outpost when built in 1803. Over the years, Michigan Avenue developed as a main thoroughfare, and today the building is one of four historic buildings, one on each corner, creating the entrance to the Michigan–Wacker Historic District.

The building "is one of the few and best examples of Beaux-Arts style classicism," according to its Chicago Landmark designation. Done with applied ornamentation and classical references, the building features a gently curved three-story entryway with paired Corinthian columns topped by an arch and a bronze relief of the fort underneath. On either side of the entry facade are griffins, or winged lions, etched into the limestone walls. A griffin was the logo of the insurance company.

The building's most prominent feature, however, is the picturesque three-story cupola that tops the 22-story tower. More columns support the dome and its plaza, which has been transformed into an outdoor eating area.

The building has had numerous tenants over the years. During the 1950s it was home to the London House jazz club, which featured nationally known musicians including Oscar Peterson, Frank Sinatra, Dave Brubeck, and Ramsey Lewis. The 452-room hotel, the result of a 21st-century restoration, takes its name from the club, long since closed.

The building was declared a Chicago Landmark in April 1996.

300 North State Street

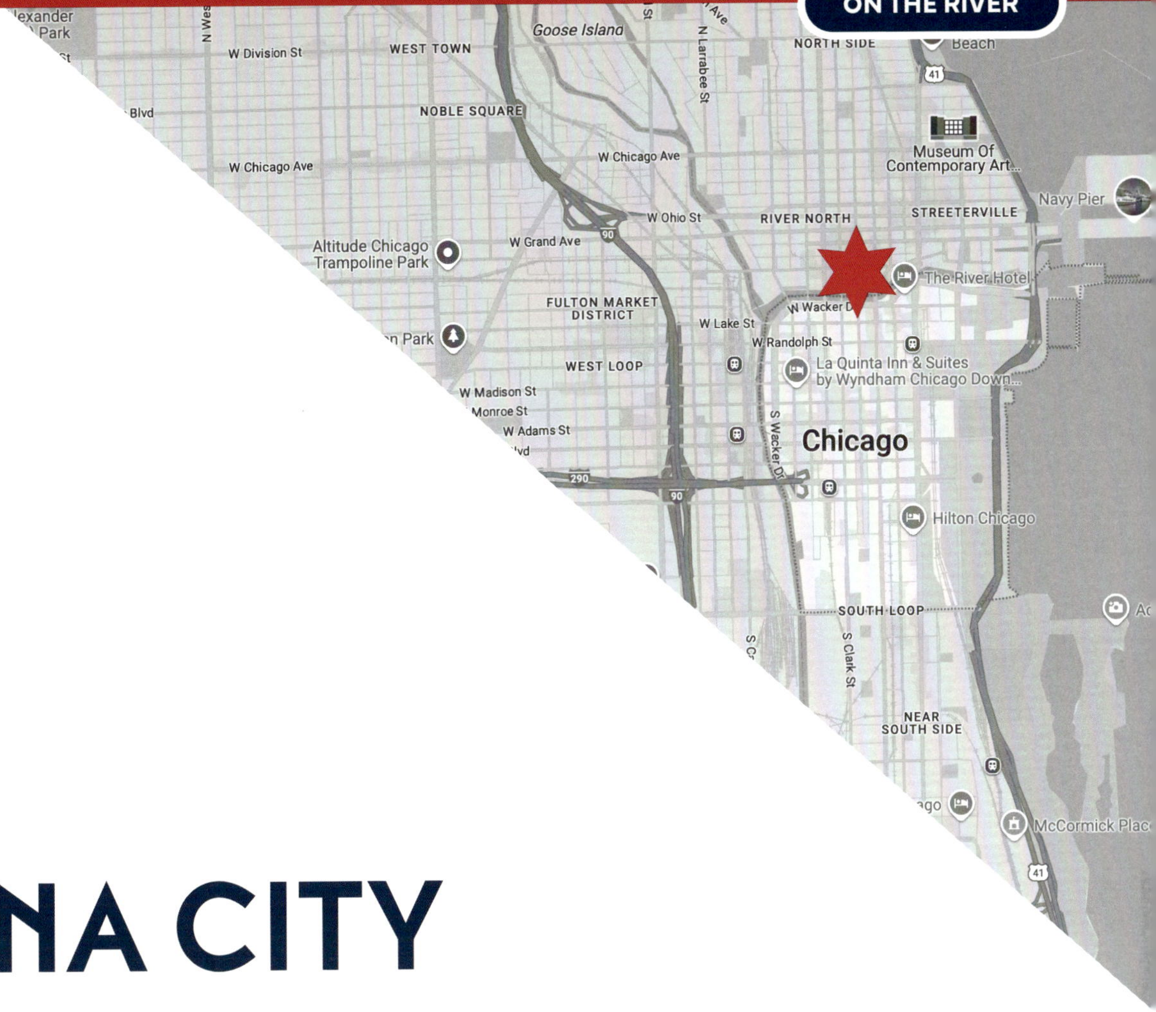

MARINA CITY

1967: Bertrand Goldberg & Associates

The circular twin buildings look like corn cobs, although architect Bertrand Goldberg called them trees with leaves. Whatever they are, today they are the symbols of Chicago—and found on souvenirs from key chains to T-shirts.

Marina City was developed as a "city within a city," the first of its kind in the nation, where people would live in a dense, urban, high-rise setting near work and be able to easily access the needed amenities of city living. The complex included residential, commercial, and entertainment uses: shops, restaurants, an ice-skating rink, a movie theater, and a bowling alley, all right at home.

In the 1950s and '60s, the city experienced substantial population flight to newly developed suburbs. Marina City, financed by a local janitorial union, was designed to entice workers to stay in the city. Goldberg was an ideal selection as architect. He believed in providing housing that was functional, inexpensive, and consistent with mass production—ideas from the Bauhaus, the German school of modern design that influenced US Modernists.

Marina City is composed of the two concrete towers rising up along the Chicago River, with the space between them filled with amenities. The original complex had 896 apartments in the two towers and a 10-story office building. Today's complex includes the two residential towers with a parking garage, restaurants, the House of Blues, and a hotel (in the old office building). At river level is the marina that gives the buildings their name. Today, most of the marina activity is for boat rentals.

The towers' concrete cores contain elevators and mechanicals. Each apartment built around a tower is pie-shaped, ending with a balcony unit of at least 225 square feet, which provides superb city vistas. Originally rentals, the building is now condominiums.

Marina City was designated a Chicago Landmark in November 2016.

433 West
Van Buren Street

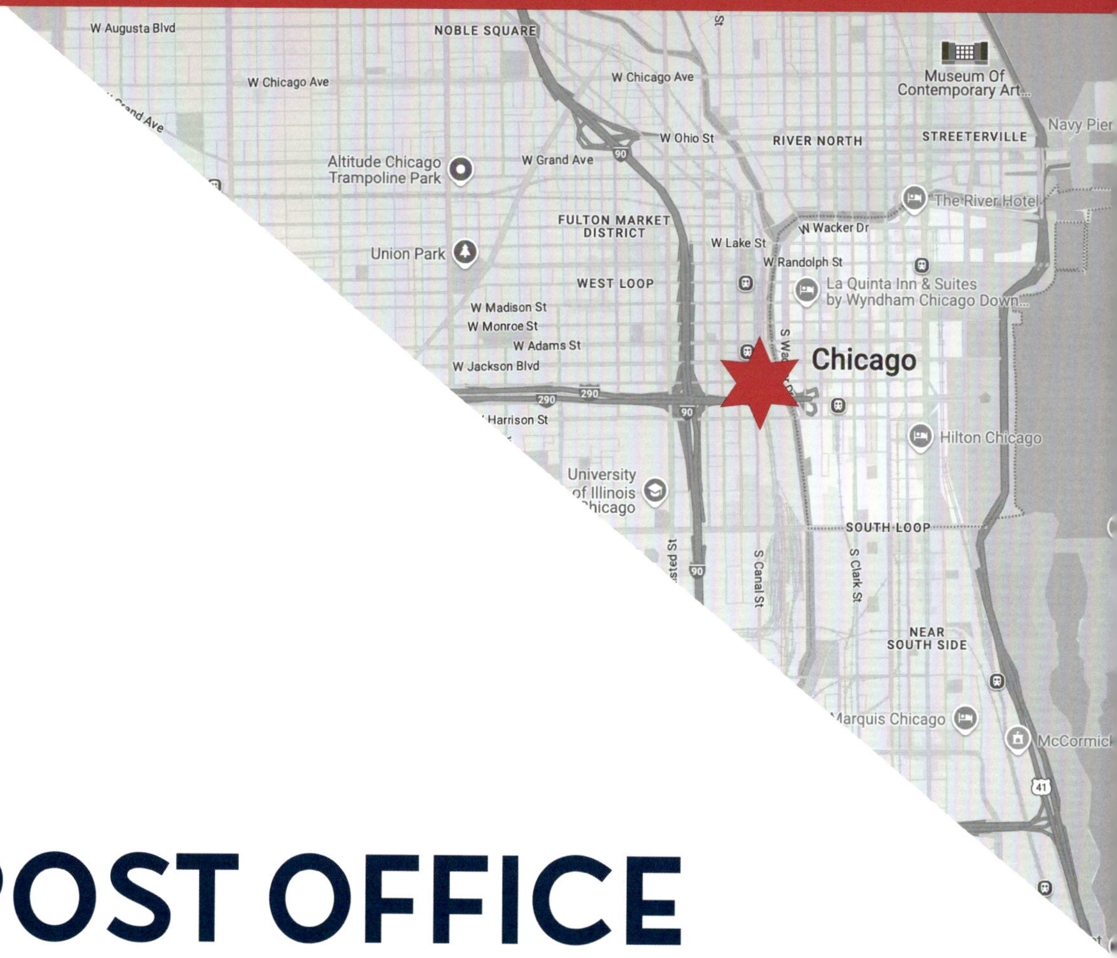

OLD POST OFFICE

1921, 1934: Graham, Anderson, Probst & White
2019: Restoration: Goettsch Partners

This nine-story building is remarkable for its massive size. It was the largest post office in the US when built. Chicago needed the huge building to process mailings from its then-extensive printing trade, which produced mail-order catalogs (Montgomery Ward's and Sears, Roebuck & Co.'s wish books among them), as well as telephone directories, all sent throughout the country.

Constructed over active railroad tracks, only a small portion of the building touches the ground. Created with an eye for the future, space was left for a highway to run underneath; Interstate 90 drove through beginning in 1955.

Also remarkable is its retrofit, transforming from post office into one of the city's best new office spaces. The post office closed in 1996, and a new one was built across the street.

Reclaiming the old building after it had been left vacant for 20 years meant a dehumidification project that sucked out enough water to fill two Olympic-size swimming pools, and the removal of asbestos and buckled wood floors. Today, the Old Post Office features both a fabulous Art Deco marble lobby from the original building plus a new 3.5-acre rooftop garden including a running track, and pickleball, tennis, and basketball courts, for the benefit of those who work inside. The massive 2.5-million-square-foot interior means no tenant rents simply an office or even a floor; spaces are measured in football-field sizes.

Today, tours given to highlight the remarkable transformation also feature historical sections including several "Stuart's Alleys," where postal inspectors hid to watch—or spy on—workers, ostensibly to prevent theft.

The building was named a Chicago Landmark in October 2017; it was added to the National Register of Historic Places in 2001. *Batman Begins* (2005) and *The Dark Knight* (2008) were filmed here.

LOADING ZONE
TOW ZONE

444 West
Lake Street

RIVER POINT

2017: Pickard Chilton, Kendall/Heaton Associates

A beauty of an office building stands tall at the westernmost end of the Chicago River's Main Stem, at the point where the South and North Branches meet. The 52-story River Point tower flaunts the most striking parts of its design: two arches, one each at the top and bottom, that together create a structural curvature required because of complications from railroad tracks.

Called eye-catching by many, the building's glass mirrors much of what is in front of it, including all the traffic along the river and its cross-river neighbor, 333 West Wacker Drive, another glass-faced building. Inside, the river-facing main lobby is three stories high. Both east and west (entrance) facades are glazed glass.

The building is set back and built over the air rights belonging to the rail lines. A green roof of a 1.5-acre terraced riverside park and plaza covers the tracks. National Amtrak and local Metra (Chicago's suburban rail system) trains as well as Blue Line Chicago Transit Authority "L" lines run underneath, through a tunnel designed to be wide enough to accommodate promised high-speed train service. The trains exhaust their fumes through porthole-shaped "windows" that in fact are fans, visible on the river side.

The structural engineering to accommodate the building and the trains, as well as a three-level parking garage, was done by Magnusson Klemencic, the firm that also engineered the nearby 150 Riverside Plaza, with the same river and railroad tracks challenges.

Installed in 2020, in front of the building in the park, is a sculpture by internationally known Spanish architect and sculptor Santiago Calatrava. Bright red, 29 feet tall, it is made of welded aluminum, and its circular shape gives it its name, *Constellation*. Some have described it as "leaflike," as "flames of a fire," or as "a dancing firebird" in the abstract.

401 East Wacker Drive

THE ST. REGIS CHICAGO

2020: Studio Gang, Jeanne Gang, lead designer; bKL Architecture, architect of record

The St. Regis is a magnificent example of vertical geometry. What looks like three towers rising from the Chicago River's south bank are, actually, "stems" coming off a single base, according to architect Jeanne Gang. To a viewer looking up from the river, the building has a fluid appearance, with a graceful, curving blue-green silhouette. The three interconnected stems rise to 47, 71, and 95 stories (above the central platform), the tallest being the farthest from Lake Michigan.

The 1.9-million-square-foot, mixed-use building houses the St. Regis Hotel in the shortest stem and 393 condominiums throughout the rest. It is Chicago's third-tallest building but, more importantly, also the world's tallest structure designed by a woman architect.

The westernmost stem has a dark, horizontal ring near the top. It is the empty 83rd "blow-through floor," installed to reduce wind-induced sway. The building also hosts six liquid tuned mass dampers, water-filled tanks whose sloshing contents likewise offset wind.

The stem design is based on a frustum, a form created by slicing off the top of a pyramid. Gang alternates the frustum, using 12-story building blocks shaped like movie theater popcorn boxes alternately—stacking an upright over an upside-down unit, giving the illusion of gradual curves. Six gradients of custom-coated greenish-blue glass clad the 101-story building. Glass color varies based on location, darkest for areas that need the most protection from the sun.

The central stem, held up by the outside two, aligns with DuSable Lake Shore and Field Drives, providing a connection to the Chicago Riverwalk. The eastern/main entrance faces the six-acre Lakeshore East Park.

The St. Regis Chicago has been lauded for transforming Chicago's skyline. Critic Vladimir Belogolovsky calls it one of the two "most original" Chicago high-rise buildings in recent years (the other being the Gang-designed Aqua) and a "21st century architectural icon."

222
MERCHANDISE MART PLAZA

THE MART

(MERCHANDISE MART)

1930: Graham, Anderson, Probst & White

The world's largest—measured by square footage—building when it was built today is the largest privately held commercial structure in the US, with approximately 4.2 million square feet of space, covering two city blocks and rising 340 feet. What began as a wholesale warehouse is today a mixed-use building housing new tech businesses, a wholesale furniture and apparel center that is the largest design center in North America, and a gathering spot with a sizeable restaurant and food court—all of which connects to a Chicago Transit Authority station.

In addition, the Mart is the "screen" upon which Art on the Mart is presented nightly during the summer months. Programs vary and include photo essays about art from local and international artists. All free, after darkness falls.

The massive limestone building, on the north side of the main stem of the Chicago River, was, when built, an outpost for Marshall Field and Co.'s wholesale business. The Art Deco–style building—with vertical lines that aid the eye in moving upward—is dotted with gold-colored diamonds embedded in limestone, and features octagonal corners and a pyramidal roof. In front, eight bronze busts, four times life-size, memorialize the nation's renowned retailers such as Field, including Frank Woolworth, Aaron Montgomery Ward, John Wanamaker, Edward Filene, and George Huntington Hartford, A&P founder.

The interior features artist Jules Guérin–designed murals in the lobby and a centralized amenity area for eating (a food court and restaurant, plus nearby seating on the wide, giant stairway) and gathering.

In 2007, the Mart received LEED-EB (Leadership in Energy and Environmental Design for Existing Buildings from the US Green Building Council) Silver recognition, the world's largest building to earn the certification signifying modernization for sustainability.

435 North Michigan Avenue

TRIBUNE TOWER RESIDENCES

(TRIBUNE TOWER)

1925: Howells and Hood

"The most beautiful office building in the world." That's what the contest was about, and this, the winner, does perhaps meet that definition. It was 1922, and the *Chicago Tribune*, a newspaper presence in the city since the 1860s, was seeking a new home.

The contest awarded $50,000 in prize money to John Mead Howells and Raymond Hood of New York. Why was their building chosen? Many surmised it was because of the Gothic gargoyles and flying buttresses that top the Art Deco–style 36-story shaft that looks for all the world like a French cathedral. The tower has a crown of open stone tracery, reminiscent of the Tour de Beurre, or Butter Tower, of the cathedral in Rouen, France. Could that be what drew editor and publisher of the *Tribune*, Col. Robert McCormick, former World War I soldier who fought in France and loved all things French, to this entry? Many think so.

Interestingly, the contest garnered 264 entries, most fostering ideas for 20th-century skyscrapers, looking forward, versus the winner's look to the past.

The building, rising up 463 feet on the north river bank, across the street from the Wrigley Building, "bookends" the entrance to Michigan Avenue, which in time became "The Magnificent (Shopping) Mile." Both buildings glow at night, Wrigley in white, Tribune in gold. Lighting is still used despite the building's 2018 transformation to residential condo units.

Embedded in the limestone walls at street level are 150 stone pieces from the world's most famous buildings—the pyramids of Egypt, the Great Wall of China, and the Alamo in Texas, for example—most brought to Chicago by the *Tribune's* foreign correspondents at Col. McCormick's bidding.

The building became a Chicago Landmark in February 1989. It also contributes to the National Register of Historic Places' Michigan–Wacker Historic District, 1978.

Chicago Tri

TRUMP

401 North Wabash Avenue

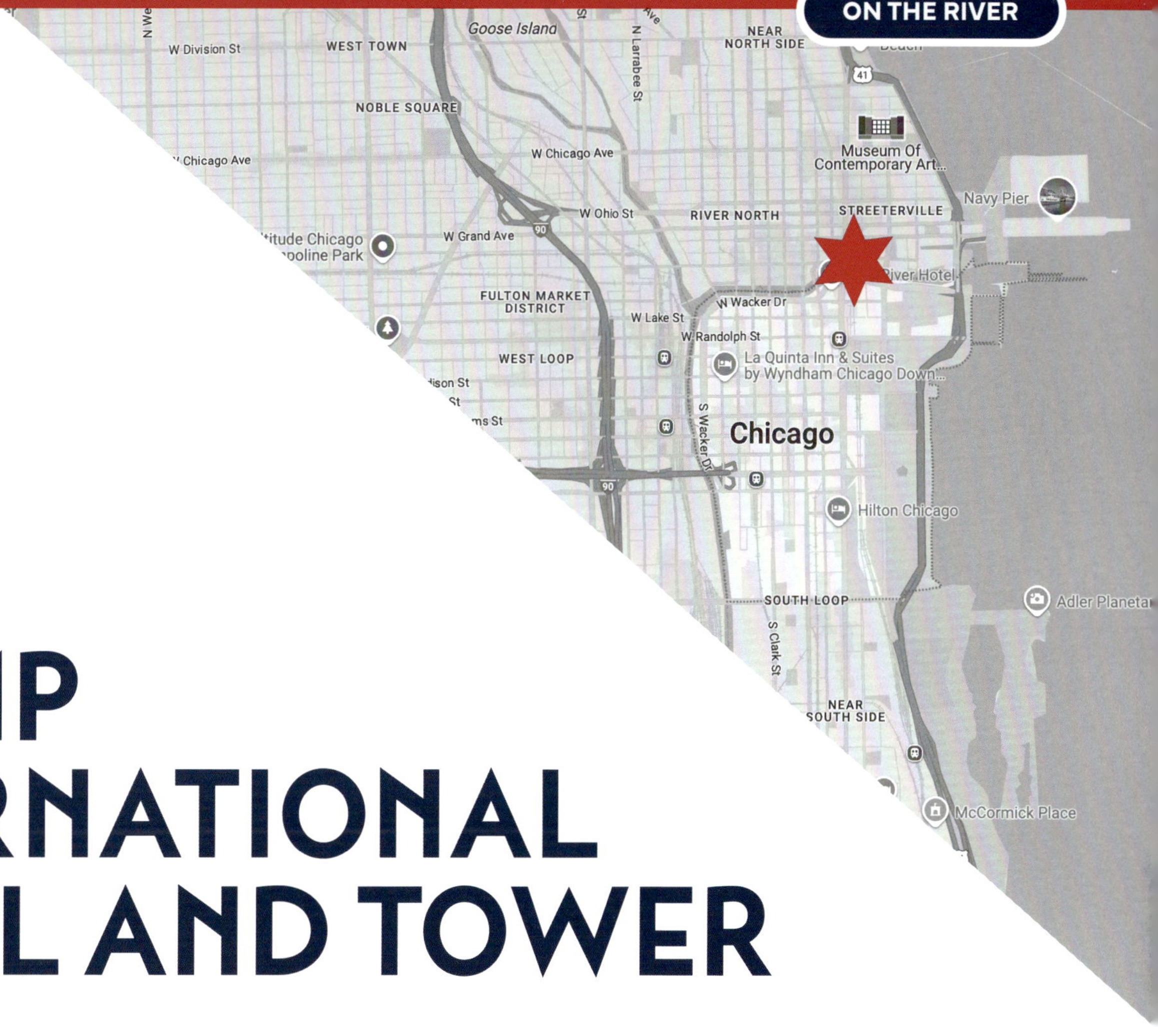

TRUMP INTERNATIONAL HOTEL AND TOWER

2009: Skidmore, Owings & Merrill, Adrian Smith lead designer

The shiny, silver-blue curved skyscraper with President Donald Trump's last name in 20-foot-high, backlit letters spread across its face (installed in 2014) was to have been the world's tallest when initially planned. Plans were scaled back after the Sept. 11 attacks to make the building less of a target for terrorists, but this is still the second-tallest in the city.

Completed in 2009, the building is mixed-use, with 486 condominiums at the top and a 339-room hotel on the center floors. Parking is included in the building, and banqueting and meeting rooms are located at the lower, Chicago River level. The building becomes slenderer as it gets taller, with a wider girth for the parking levels than the condo units.

The building was designed by architect Adrian Smith, who later designed today's world's-tallest building, the Burj Khalifa in Dubai, UAE, with design lines not unlike Chicago's tower. The Chicago building is constructed of concrete, rather than steel. That reduced costs, minimized sway, and maximized window space. When completed, the building at the curve in the Chicago River was the largest reinforced concrete building in North America. The curved shape and silvery-blue stainless steel, aluminum, and glass curtain wall were intended to reflect both the river's color and curvature.

The concrete core, which holds the building's mechanicals, is reinforced by horizontal outriggers that connect to exterior columns. This core-and-outrigger construction is often compared to how a skier uses poles to maintain balance. The non-reflective glass that was used is bird-friendly.

The 227-foot spire was added to the building reportedly at the request of then-mayor Richard M. Daley. The skyscraper hit headlines in 2020 when a man dangled from the 16th floor demanding an audience with the then-president, before being taken into custody.

233 South Wacker Drive

WILLIS TOWER

(SEARS TOWER)

1974: Skidmore, Owings & Merrill, Bruce Graham, architect, Fazlur Khan, engineer

The world's tallest building for 20 years, yet today not even in the Top 20, the Willis/Sears Tower is still tallest for Chicagoans. The era's greatest structural achievement paved the way for skyscrapers worldwide, including those that eventually topped the tower.

Designed for Sears, Roebuck & Co., at the time the largest retailer in the US, the tower, one of the last of the city's major Mid-Century Modern designs, capped Chicago's drive for the biggest and best. At 110 stories—the highest the Federal Aviation Administration would allow—the unique structure was developed by engineer Fazlur Khan. Called "bundled tube construction," the building is created out of nine "tubes," each a column-free module measuring 75 feet by 75 feet, all of which rise 50 floors, when two drop off, followed by two more at floor 66 and three at floor 90. The remaining two are the full 110 stories. Setbacks created by the elimination of some tubes of the black anodized aluminum with bronze-tinted glass walls create the tower's distinctive profile.

The building plaza for years was windswept and difficult to access, but that has been remedied recently with entry renovations and the introduction at the base of a multistory food court called the Catalog after Sears's famous wish book.

The building's site was chosen for easy public transportation access to all city areas for all Sears employees. While many Chicagoans still call it Sears, naming rights since 2009 have belonged to Willis Group Holdings, a global insurance broker.

The symbolism—tallest in the city, formerly tallest in the world—is certainly excellent, but many critics call it a structural engineering triumph rather than an architectural accomplishment. Still, visitors enjoy breathtaking vistas from the Skydeck Chicago, 1,353 feet up, and the building more than holds its own, making a strong statement in a crowded skyline.

410 North Michigan Avenue

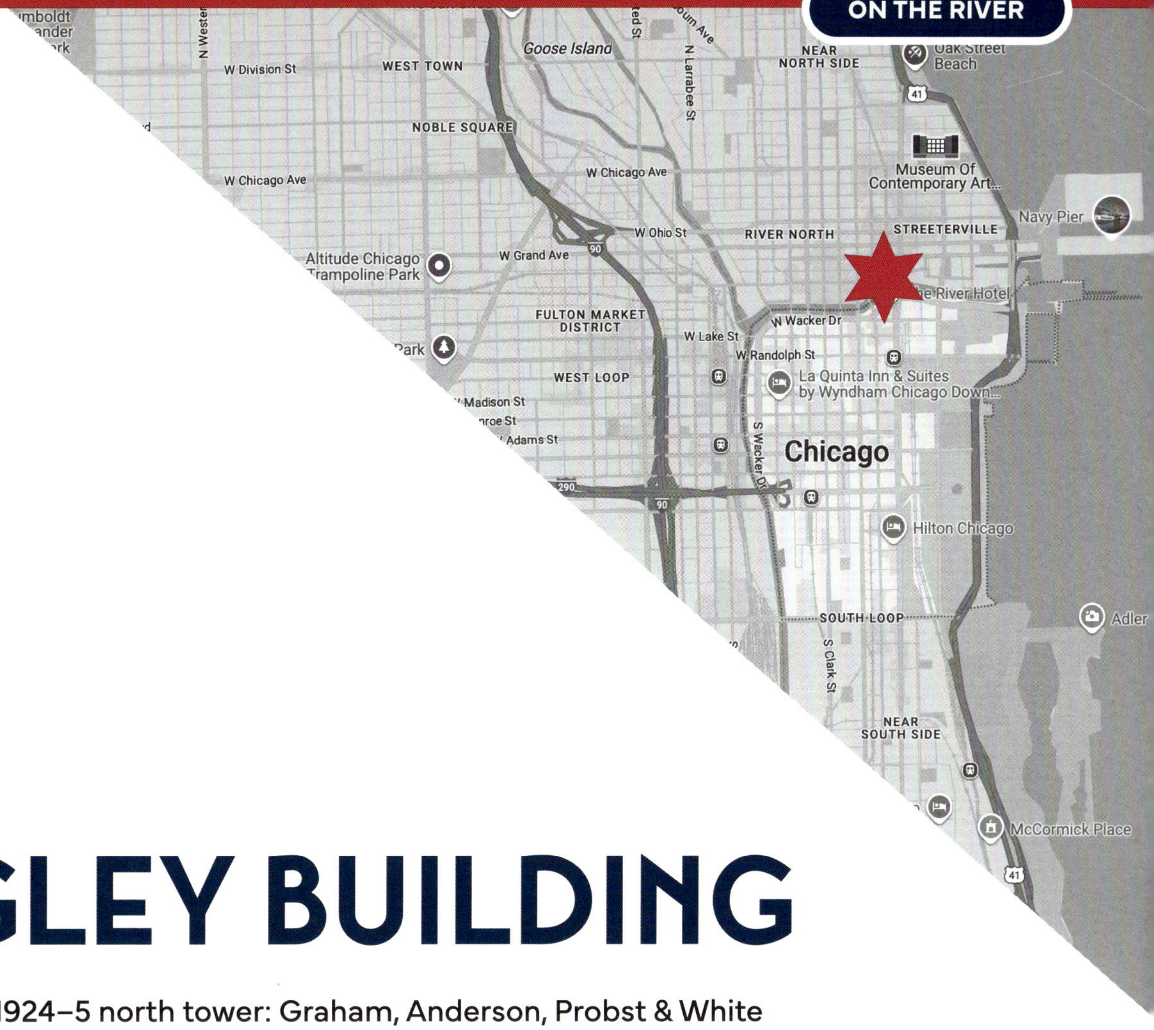

WRIGLEY BUILDING

1919–22 south tower; 1924–5 north tower: Graham, Anderson, Probst & White

Gleaming in the spotlights of evening, the Wrigley Building shines as white as the toothy smiles in chewing gum advertisements. This, the former corporate headquarters for the Wrigley Company, is often called "the building that gum built." It is one of Chicago's favorite landmarks, a photo op few tourists miss.

The first building erected north of the Chicago River following the construction of the Michigan Avenue bridge in 1920, the Wrigley Building was reminiscent of the buildings found at the 1893 World's Columbian Exposition (Fair), which impressed the company founder. William Wrigley Jr. came to Chicago as a soap and later baking soda salesman, unsuccessful at both. But when he put free gum on each product box, sales skyrocketed. He quickly pivoted to producing and selling chewing gum, introducing Juicy Fruit and Spearmint brands at the fair.

Created in the Beaux Arts style, with ornamentation all over and especially along the top cornice, the building is a steel-framed skyscraper clad in Indiana limestone and white terra-cotta. Six shades of white are used, from blue-white at the bottom, getting whiter and brighter to creamy-white at the top. Terra-cotta translates as "baked earth"; it is clay baked for days in molds in a kiln at high temperatures. Terra-cotta is fire resistant, a welcomed cladding in Chicago, which experienced a catastrophic fire in 1871.

The building has a historic antecedent for the 11-story clock tower on the south tower; it is modeled after the Giralda Tower in Seville, Spain. The building and its across-the-street neighbor, Tribune Tower Residences, were the original "bookends" of Michigan Avenue when the Michigan Avenue Bridge was built. When extended northward, Michigan Avenue (formerly Pine Street) became home to high-end retail and was ultimately dubbed "The Magnificent Mile."

The Wrigley Building became a Chicago Landmark in February 2012.

860-880 LAKE SHORE DRIVE

1949–52: Ludwig Mies van der Rohe; PACE Associates and Holsman, Holsman, Klekamp & Taylor, associate architects

One of the most famous apartment complexes in the world, these two 26-story towers are generally regarded as the most perfect expression of the high-rise steel-framed structure. While today they look at home in the skyline with similar Modernist buildings, when built these two were revolutionary. Because of the ubiquitousness of glass-and-steel buildings, it is almost impossible to appreciate their initial impact.

Architect Ludwig Mies van der Rohe came to Chicago from Germany in the 1930s, having headed Germany's Bauhaus school of modern art, which was shuttered by order of the Nazis. Mies, already famous in Europe for his Modern style, took the position of dean of the School of Architecture at Chicago's Armour Institute, later Illinois Institute of Technology and today's Illinois Tech. There, he trained an entire generation of architects.

In 1946, working from his private practice, Mies teamed with developer Herbert Greenwald to create the Promontory Point apartments in Hyde Park. Both men believed in simplicity of structure, streel-frame technology, and sophisticated high-rise living. The era of postwar residential living began when, in 1949, Mies—again working with Greenwald—designed 860–880 North Lake Shore Drive.

The steel frame—columns and beams—was covered with black painted steel plates, a result of the city-required fireproofing. Welded to the frame are vertical I-beams, eight inches deep, which rise from the second story to the roofline, 250 feet up, emphasizing the buildings' verticality. When seen from the street, the buildings reflect both one another and buildings around them. The towers' siting offers optimal views for residents. The 860 building has four apartments per floor, while 880 has six.

The buildings were added to the National Register of Historic Places in 1980, named a Chicago Landmark in 1996, and became a National Historic Landmark the same year.

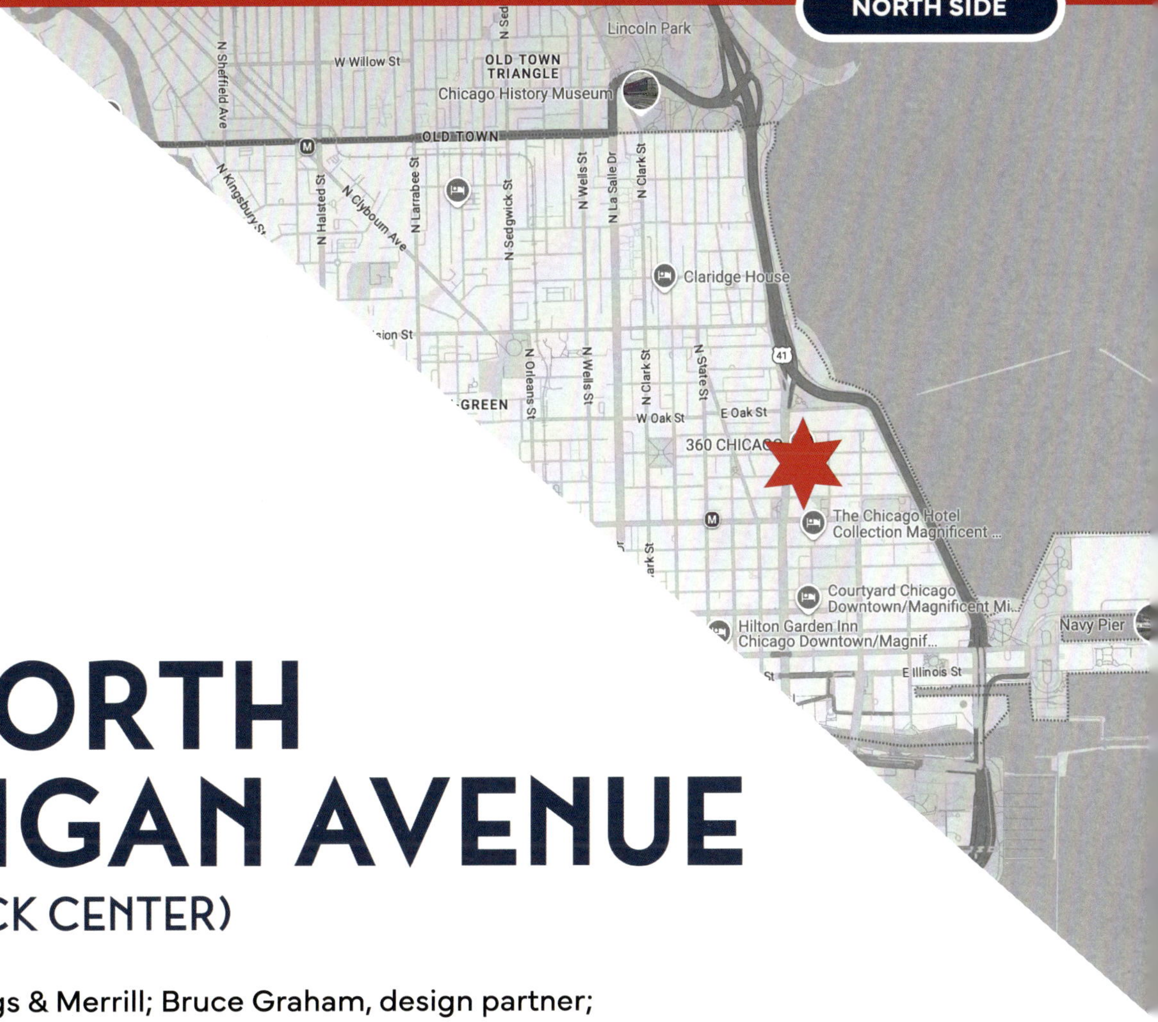

875 NORTH MICHIGAN AVENUE

(JOHN HANCOCK CENTER)

1969: Skidmore, Owings & Merrill; Bruce Graham, design partner; Fazlur Khan, senior project engineer

Epitomizing poet Carl Sandburg's words, "Big John," as it was called when it first went up, this building illustrates how Chicago is the city of "big shoulders." Bold and brawny, this skyscraper also is indicative of Chicago's love affair with Modernism—the glass and steel buildings of the mid-century with sleek lines and no applied ornamentation that always reached higher.

A Chicago favorite, the building illustrates the changeover from brick or stone-clad buildings to the Mid-Century Modernist styles of the post–World War II era, and continues Chicago's proud heritage of fostering new, innovative architectural styles. The super-tall building not only punctuates the skyline, particularly when viewed coming from the north, it also houses a 94th-floor observation deck with spectacular panoramic views. The architect-engineer team that later would be responsible for the Sears/Willis Tower worked together here first.

The 100-story mixed-use Modernist building is clad in black anodized aluminum and tinted glass, with a profile that tapers as it rises. That form allows for larger floor areas for the retail, offices, and parking that fill the lower levels and smaller floor plates for the residential living found higher up, floors 44–93. The obelisk form references ancient Egypt and the Washington Monument, symbolizing stability and staying power.

Huge steel cross-braces, part of an exoskeleton indicating how the building withstands the wind, go across windows. Initially it was feared that residents would not want to live in units with windows blocked by the braces, but unexpectedly residents sought to purchase those units, taking pride in living with a window "X."

The building, the colossus of Michigan Avenue, was renamed by its address in 2018, but Chicagoans still use the Hancock moniker. Many, in fact, still think the Hancock is Chicago's tallest building. It actually is only the fifth tallest today.

3601 NORTH MILWAUKEE AVENUE

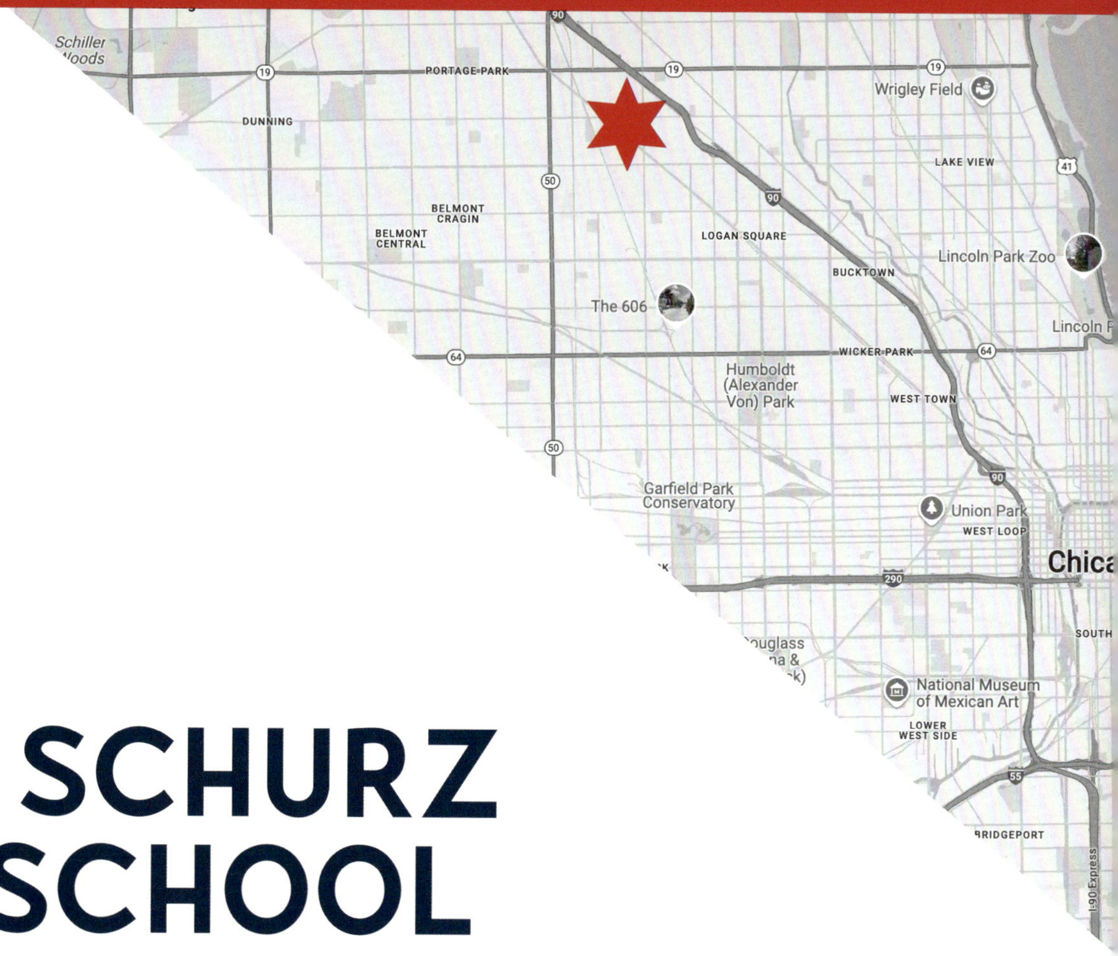

CARL SCHURZ HIGH SCHOOL

1909: Dwight H. Perkins
1914: Addition: Arthur F. Hussander; 1924: Addition: John C. Christensen

Dwight Perkins, called the "father of school architecture," triumphed with this design for Carl Schurz High School. It is a dramatic composition of soaring vertical walls topped with deep overhangs of high-pitched, gabled roofs. The two-toned colored, so-called polychromatic, bricks make the huge building especially impressive.

In 1905, Perkins was appointed as the chief architect for the Chicago Board of Education. During his tenure he created designs for more than 40 schools. Schurz was his acknowledged masterpiece. When Perkins worked as school architect, the Board of Education was headed by famed settlement house founder Jane Addams. Both wanted to aid the assimilation of immigrants into American society by providing interesting, well-lighted environments for learning.

Schurz represents a mix of two architectural styles. The strong vertical piers are characteristic of Chicago's rising commercial buildings, while the overhanging roof, detailed brickwork, and strong geometric forms are elements often identified with Prairie-style design. Here, Prairie vocabulary, usually found only on residential buildings, is utilized for an institutional building.

Perkins enjoyed experimenting with interlocking forms. Using reddish-orange and burnt-brown segments, he made the vertical lines pop. The red tile roof adds more color. The entire complex is fronted by a great lawn. Later additions/wings by other architects followed Perkins's design. Perkins himself reused his own plans. Schurz has a "twin," Bowen High School on the city's south side.

The school is named in honor of a German-born journalist and political leader. Schurz was listed on the National Register of Historic Places in February 2011, having been designated as a Chicago Landmark in December 1979. A 1994–96 renovation by Ross Barney + Jankowski restored the clay tile roof and revealed its original color scheme.

UNITED STATES
POSTAL SERVICE

1365 North Astor Street

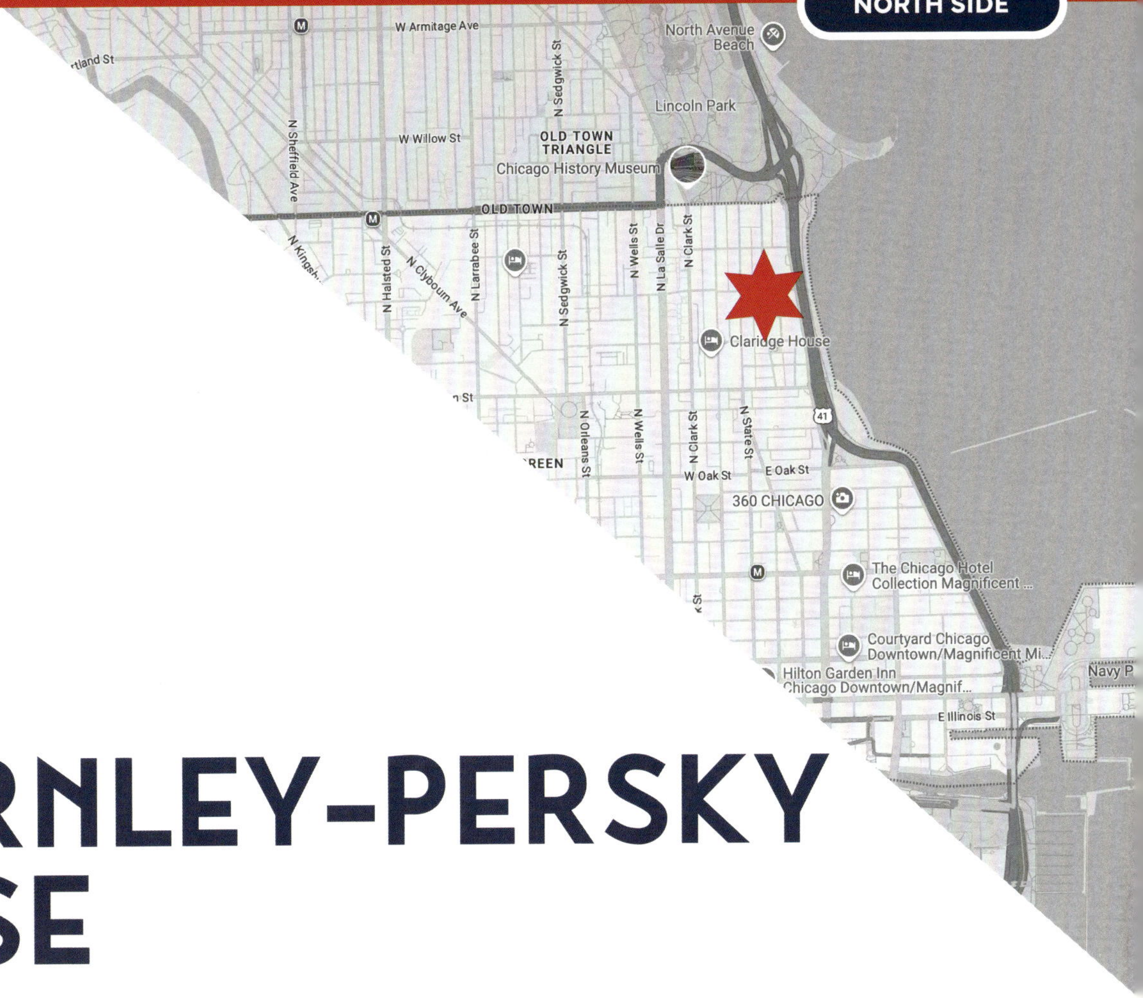

CHARNLEY-PERSKY HOUSE

1892: Adler & Sullivan

This three-story house at the corner of Astor and Schiller Streets has been credited to both Louis Sullivan and his draftsman, Frank Lloyd Wright. A house with designs from both fathers of American architecture is unique, although Sullivan takes the majority of the credit.

The home's tenant and owner, the Society of Architectural Historians, calls it a "pivotal work of modern architecture." The home illustrates Sullivan's search for an American style, breaking the tradition of copying European trends.

The Gold Coast neighborhood was known then and now for its wealthy homeowners. Charnley House broke neighborhood traditions; it is not a traditional multistoried Victorian. Instead, it is designed in block forms, abstract squares, and rectangles, creating a forerunner to today's modern, more horizontal residences.

Orange-brown Roman (thin) brick clads the lower floors, with cut limestone around the front door and edges. A lighter, wood-with-limestone trimmed balcony fronts the upper floors. Sullivan-esque designs illuminate the base below the columned loggia, an arcade-like balcony, open on one side.

The interior features a spectacular atrium in the center that rises from street level to roof level and houses a lofty wooden staircase. Interior ornamentation illustrates Sullivan's love of geometric forms intertwined with plants. The 11-room house has wood trim in the living and dining rooms and the library, noteworthy for Sullivan's leaf designs.

Built by James Charnley, an 1890s lumber baron, in 1995 it was sold to the Seymour H. Persky Foundation, which donated the Charnley House to the SAH for its national headquarters. The house name was changed when the society moved to Chicago.

The home became a Chicago Landmark in 1972. It was named to the National Register of Historic Places in April 1970 and designated a National Historic Landmark in August 1998.

2750 NORTH LAKEVIEW AVENUE

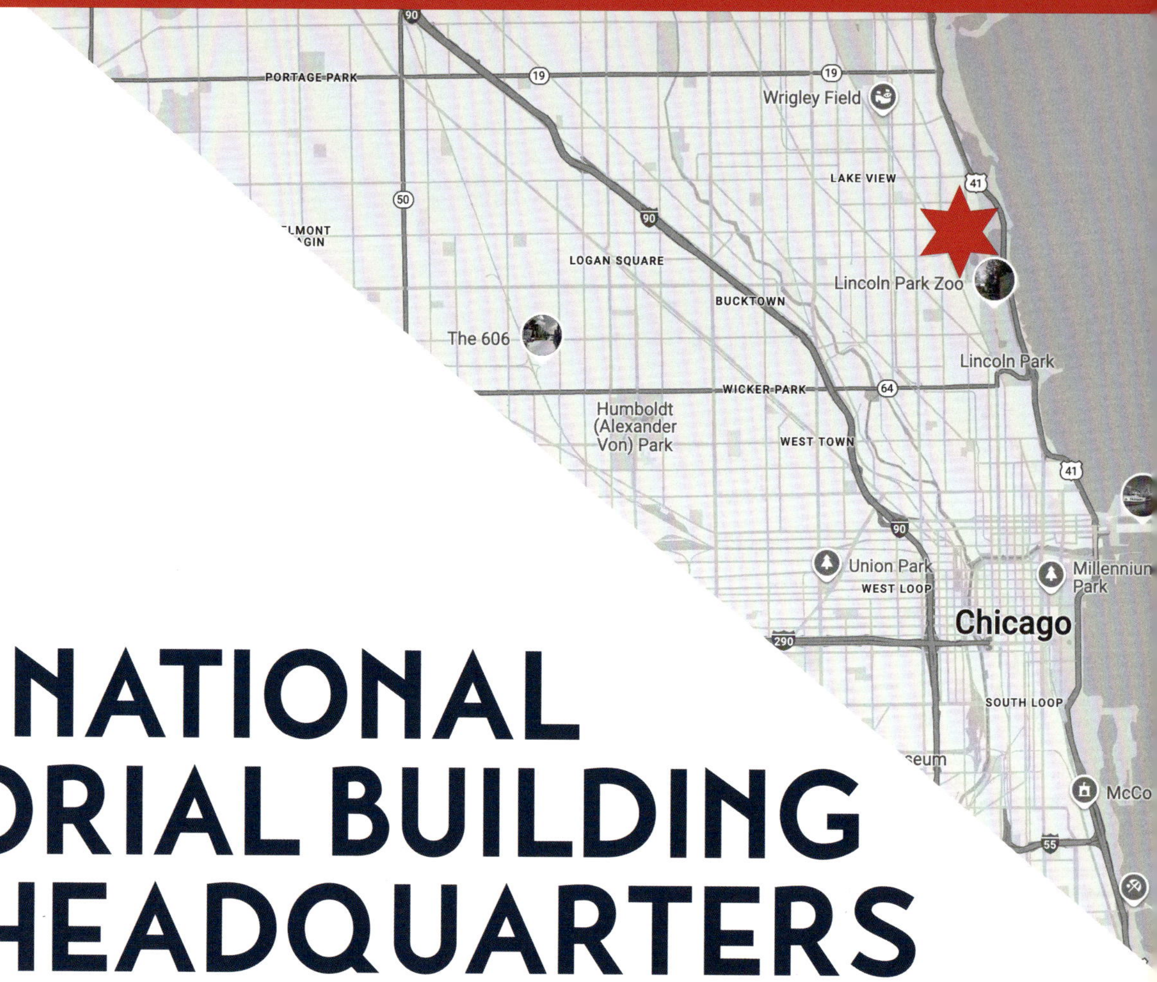

ELKS NATIONAL MEMORIAL BUILDING AND HEADQUARTERS

1924–26: Main building, Egerton Swartwout

The elegance of this building begins with its interesting circular shape, domed top, and strong position on the corner of Lakeview Avenue and Diversey Street, facing Lincoln Park. But even adding the sculpted life-sized elks by artist Laura Gardin Fraser in front cannot prepare you for the exuberance and artistry of the grand interior.

Built as a monument to members of the Benevolent and Protective Order of Elks, more than 1,000 of whom died in World War I, it today has been rededicated to honor all fallen Elks in World War II, Korea, and Vietnam. The memorial's interior features a massive two-story rotunda with colorful marble walls highlighted with a plethora of murals and sculptures.

It is a grand commemoration building, an exceptional example of a monumental building in the Beaux Arts style, emphasizing ornamentation. The dome reaches 100 feet above the floor.

The building is the creation of New York architect Egerton Swartwout. His Roman-inspired dome, designed with a 38-foot-high colonnade that rises from a frieze (a decorative horizontal band near the ceiling) carved in high relief is impressive.

But work in the interior also wows! Allegorical mural artists Eugene Savage and Edwin H. Blashfield created the *Sermon on the Mount* mosaic. Adolph A. Weinman's sculptures in the wall niches depict traits such as "brotherhood" and "charity." James Fraser's entry sculptures complete the artwork collection that together create a riotously colorful interior.

Swartwout was selected from a competition to create both a memorial and a national headquarters for the Elks (founded in 1868 and still going strong), which "would inspire Elks and captivate the public." The mission was obviously fulfilled, as this memorial is nothing short of awe-inspiring.

Elks Memorial was named a Chicago Landmark in October 2003.

FIDELITY

4022
P
PAY AT PAY BOX
ParkChicago
458 117
4024

4024 North
Elston Avenue

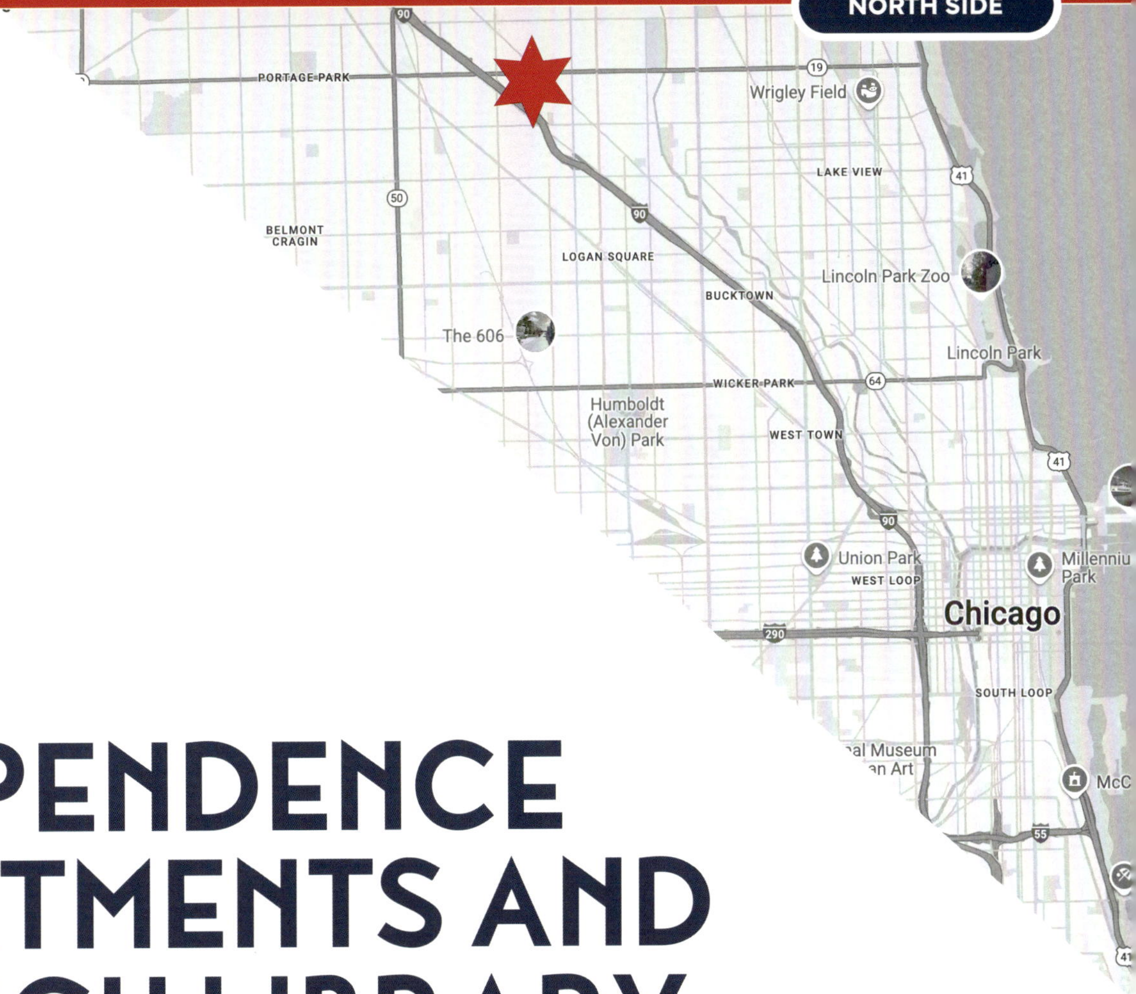

INDEPENDENCE APARTMENTS AND BRANCH LIBRARY

2019: John Ronan Architects

This is one of three experimental mixes of Chicago public libraries with affordable housing. This white box with terraces surrounded by assorted colors tops a two-story gray building base with the word "Independence" incised on it. It is welcoming, both to those who live there and to anyone who wants to borrow a book.

In 2017, the Chicago Housing Authority and the Chicago Public Library joined forces to pair mixed-income housing with libraries. Called colocations, they are a combination of two building types: library on the street level and housing above. Each of the three buildings completed is individual and worth a visit, but this one stands out with its colorful facade. Architect John Ronan, known for other interesting buildings that also celebrate color, indicated that the surrounds on the front of the white facade are placed to give each occupant pride in his/her unit. The color scheme is carried into the interior, where doorframes, entry doors, and the floors in front of the entries are done in the same color.

The library facade is created from dark stone panels at the top and tinted, highly reflective glass on the bottom. Natural light floods the two-story interior. The second floor abuts the accessible green roof that tops the parking garage. The four-story building steps back from the sidewalk, its housing unit height behind the library section, which sits closer to the sidewalk. The library's two-story height fits in with its neighbors along the street.

Inside, the white-with-colors scheme is followed again, with colorful upholstered stools, rugs, and chairs splashing against the white walls and lighting fixtures. A bleacher-style stairway functions as an informal meeting area, but there is also a community multipurpose room.

NORTH SIDE

600 NORTH CLARK STREET

MCDONALD'S CHICAGO FLAGSHIP RESTAURANT

2018: Ross Barney Architects

McDonald's belongs to Chicago. The first McDonald's, the franchise known by its golden arches, opened in nearby suburban Des Plaines, and McDonald's recently moved its corporate headquarters into the city.

In 2002, McDonald's commissioned Ross Barney Architects to upgrade its busiest city operation. The architects ran with the idea from a simple redo to creating a spectacularly sustainable fast-food operation—while opening the door for others to do similarly at any of its 40,000 worldwide McDonald's locations.

McDonald's Chicago flagship does not drop the traditional golden arches. Rather it incorporates them structurally into the new prototype. Believing that the most sustainable building is one that already exists, the architects retained the existing kitchen and basement and reclad existing walls.

A roof or pergola of solar panels provides 55 percent of the 19,000-square-foot building's electricity needs. Beneath this "big roof," indoor dining areas connect to outdoor plazas with permeable pavers that absorb water. In the interior dining room, new materials were used for the first time in a Chicago commercial building: Cross-laminated timber (CLT) and glulam beams, chosen for their low-embodied energy, are set against a backdrop of white birch trees planted in a suspended atri-um and hanging "plant tapestries." An understory is of edible plants; the "tapestries" improve indoor air quality and quiet the room.

Before the redo, 90 percent of the building was surrounded with parking. The new configuration provides for a 72 percent increase in pedestrian-focused areas—still keeping some parking and drive-through.

You can see the rooftop farm through a clerestory (high) window. Planted with apple trees, a variety of lettuces, broccoli, chives, and carrots, harvested produce is donated to the local Ronald McDonald House.

More than 70 trees dot the site, native and drought-resilient species interspersed between permeable pavers, to minimize irrigation and reduce storm-water runoff.

EXIT

neiu.edu

3390 North Avondale Avenue

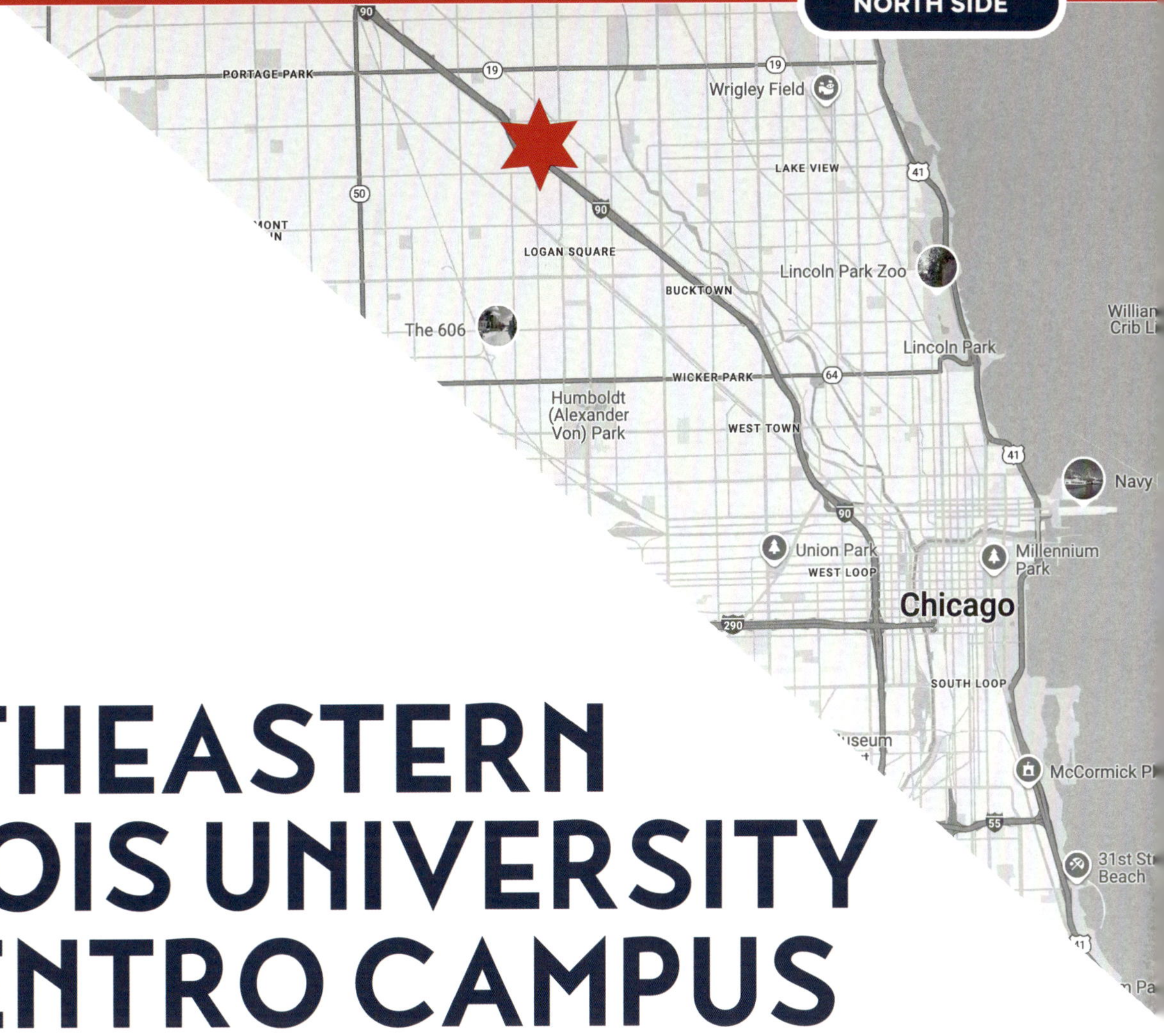

NORTHEASTERN ILLINOIS UNIVERSITY EL CENTRO CAMPUS

2014: JGMA

Is it blue? Yes, looking from one direction, but no, looking from the other. There it is yellow. Actually, the fins that point out of this building are both blue and yellow, the university's school colors, painted one on each side. With the building's arc-like curve, it whizzes by in a whirl of colors to the hundreds of thousands of drivers who pass it daily on the Kennedy Expressway traveling through the city or out to the airport.

The 66,000-square-foot El Centro Campus building of Northeastern Illinois University is designed in the Post-Modern style—a glass and steel construction of classrooms, library, and reading rooms on the inside, adding color and whimsy, and definitely sitting contextually in its place. On the exterior, the building is "sculptural. It grabs your attention . . . (it's) in motion," said former *Chicago Tribune* architecture critic Blair Kamin in a TV interview. The building's colorful nature is also a reflection of its Latino cultural heritage, brought to the design by architect Juan Moreno, JGMA president and founder.

El Centro is one of Northeastern's four locations. Founded in the 1960s to provide access and education opportunities to the Latinx community, the El Centro campus also seeks to revitalize the swath of industrial land bordered by Kimball Avenue, the Union Pacific/Northwest Metra line, and the Kennedy Expressway, serving as a catalyst for further development.

Glass walls provide views out to both the neighborhood and the expressway, but the classrooms are set back behind the long corridors along the outer walls that buffer the traffic sounds. The building is used for university classes, but hopes are there for it to become a community resource for the neighborhood as well.

Kamin's TV interview was titled "Flash and Fins." That description fits very well.

NORTH SIDE

61 WEST
SUPERIOR STREET

THE POETRY FOUNDATION

2011: John Ronan Architects

An elegant low-slung building, this one is hard to read from the street, protected as it is by a wall of perforated metal. But once you step inside to first the outer courtyard and then into the interior, it is light, airy, and decidedly dedicated to the art of the poem.

Architect John Ronan uses a multitude of materials here, beginning with the gray, punctuated, oxidized zinc screen outer wall. In the outer courtyard, he chose glass and for the interior used blond birchwood. All combine to give the building its airy, transparent appearance. Exhibits are ongoing and in summer months often flow to the outside courtyard. The building is typical of Ronan's work, with interlocking forms, an architecture that the Chicago Architecture Center says "unfolds as you walk through it."

The understated nature of the Contemporary architecture allows poetry to do the talking. A 30,000-volume library, an exhibition gallery, and a reading room are inside, with a huge portrait of the original editor and founder of *Poetry* magazine, Harriet Monroe, overseeing the enterprise.

Established in 2003, the Poetry Foundation is dedicated to bringing poetry more into the mainstream of American life. Originally located in the Fine Arts Building, the magazine Monroe founded dates from 1912. Through the years, it was known for early publishing of poets who later gained significant notoriety, such as T. S. Eliot, Robert Frost, Gwendolyn Brooks, and Langston Hughes—many if not most of the poets who are required reading in high school English. But finances were always difficult.

In 2001, the magazine received a windfall $200 million gift from Ruth Lilly, heiress to the Eli Lilly pharmaceutical fortune. That spurred creation of the Poetry Foundation, and the ability to create this permanent home.

61

10000 West Balmoral Avenue

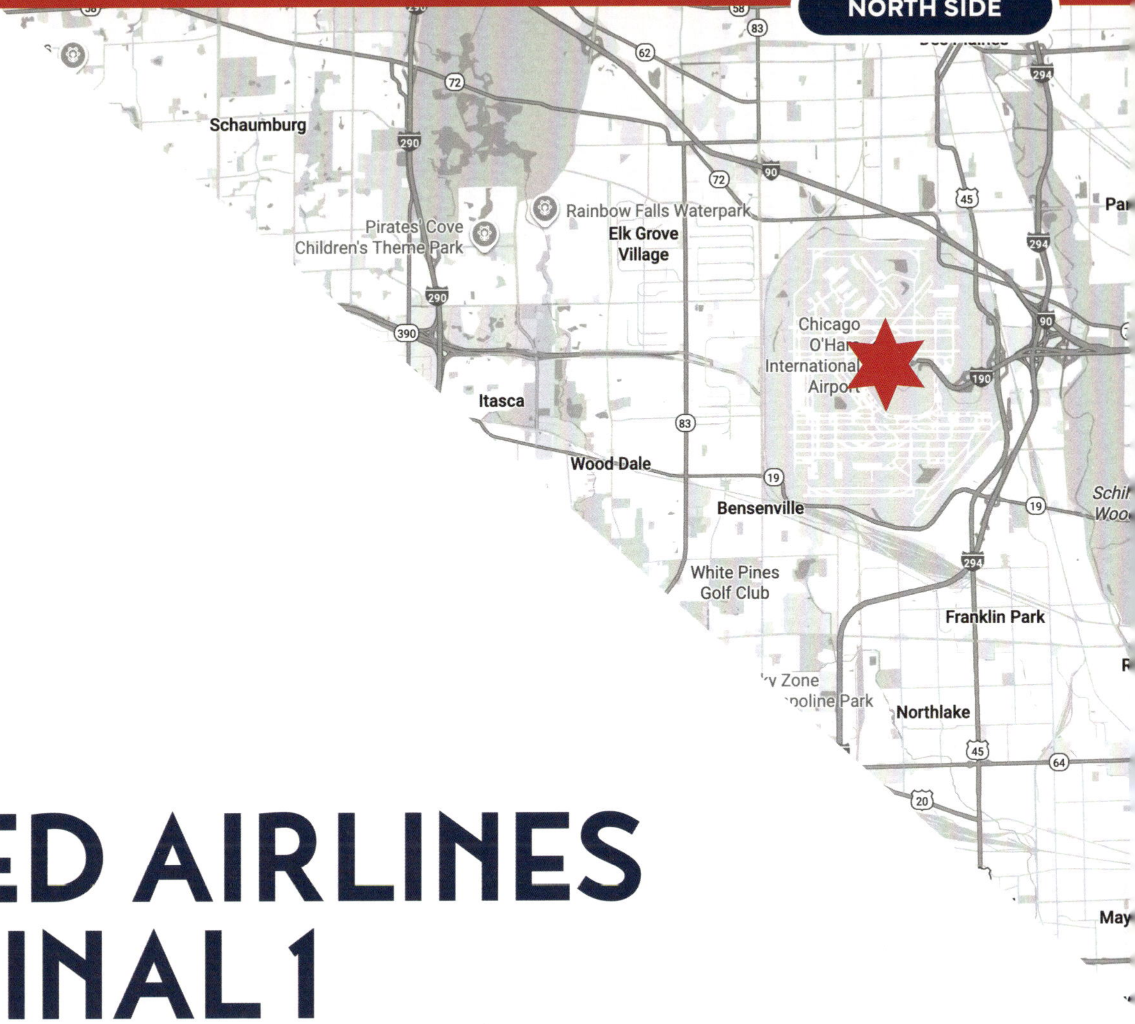

UNITED AIRLINES TERMINAL 1

1988: Helmut Jahn, Murphy/Jahn; A. Epstein & Sons, associate architects

It almost makes air travel bearable. This United Airlines Terminal from more than three decades ago still shines. As historian Robert Bruegmann says, the terminal "is that rarest of species, an instant landmark conspicuously singular, and clearly an expression of its time . . . and function."

On the street level the terminal, or concourse, is a steel-and-glass building of monumental size, allowing light to flow through humongous windows into the interior. The steel frame that holds the glass creates a free span of 120 feet, topped with 50-foot-high skylights. It is estimated that natural light can totally illuminate the area if the day is sunny enough.

And, there actually are two terminals. The second, across a wide area used for plane taxiing and parking, runs parallel to the first. Together the terminals provide 1.2 million square feet for ticketing, security, and gate waiting areas.

It has been suggested by many that architect Helmet Jahn's inspiration for the terminals was the waiting rooms of Victorian railroad sheds built with visible iron and glass skeletons. The terminal's interior vaults, asymmetrical arches, are highlighted by curved steel beams placed 30 feet apart. White and perforated with circular holes, the beams bespeak lightness again and transparency.

The 52-foot-wide and 812-foot-long pedway, or connector between the two terminals, is incredible; it is underground, it shines, and—literally—it sings. The connector, 35 feet below the ground, accessible by escalator, takes passengers into a new world: Standing on one of the four moving walkways, travelers look up to a ceiling sculpture of neon lights that change colors randomly, backed by a mirrored surface, created by artist Michael Hayden, called *Thinking Lightly.* It is synchronized with music, frequently George Gershwin's "Rhapsody in Blue."

806 North Michigan Avenue

CHICAGO WATER TOWER

1869: William W. Boyington

Built to provide clean water to city dwellers, the Chicago Water Tower, the second oldest in the nation, has evolved into the symbol of Chicago's "I Will" spirit. It is a reminder of how the city survived and rebuilt following the 1871 Great Chicago Fire.

The 154-foot-tall tower that resembles a medieval fortress housed a 138-foot vertical water pipe that, together with the Water Works, now Pumping Station, across the street, constituted the city's water distribution system. No machinery was located in the tower. The pipe was removed when it was no longer needed. Today, the tower is home to an art gallery and visitor center.

Because the tower was built of local yellow-hued Joliet limestone and metal, it was fireproof. Only charred by the flames, the tower is one of only a few buildings that withstood the fire. Chicagoans see the Water Tower as a city icon—rising from the ashes—and plaster its image on magnets, key chains, and T-shirts. Yet one visitor, the English playwright Oscar Wilde, was obviously unimpressed, famously calling it "a castellated monstrosity with pepper boxes stuck all over it."

W. W. Boyington, one of Chicago's first architects, designed the Joliet prison (1858) and Rosehill Cemetery entrance (1864) before the Water Tower—all in the Gothic Medieval style with a castellated (repeated square indentations like those on a battlement) roof and slit windows for use by long-forgotten archers.

Surviving the fire did not guarantee permanent preservation; the Tower survived several demolition threats. In 1913 planners were trying to improve Michigan Avenue traffic, while in 1948 arts groups sought space for a community center. In 1971, the Water Tower was declared a City of Chicago Landmark. In 2014, the gardens at the base of the tower were dedicated as Jane Byrne Park, honoring the former mayor.

WRIGLEY FIELD
HOME OF
CHICAGO CUBS
BOSCH POWER TOOLS
TOYOTA
GATE
3

1060 West Addison Street

WRIGLEY FIELD

1914: Zachary Taylor Davis

Steel-framed, brick-enclosed structures fit for a ballpark. That was architect Zachary Taylor Davis's reputation. He designed both the original Comiskey Park (1910) on Chicago's South Side and Wrigley Field (1914), then-modern ballparks that were intended to be permanent.

Comiskey is long gone, but Wrigley still stands, first in the hearts of ever-hopeful Cubs fans and most recently as the center of a massive renovation of the field and its neighborhood.

Chicagoans cherish the "friendly confines," as Wrigley has been known for decades. Throughout years of the Cubs' mediocre play, fans have loyally turned out to enjoy the wind blowing over Waveland Avenue, the ivy and Virginia creeper on the back brick walls, and Chicago-style hot dogs.

The original 1914 stadium was named Weeghman Park, after the owner of the Federal League Chicago Whales. The Whales lasted a year, but the stadium kept the name even after the Chicago Cubs, a Major League team, arrived in 1916. Chewing gum magnate William Wrigley Jr. took control of the Cubs in 1921 and named the field Cubs Park. In 1926 the name was changed to Wrigley. It is the oldest park in the National League and second oldest in the majors, after Boston's Fenway Park (1912). Enlargements came over the years, including the famous centerfield bleachers and scoreboard in 1937–8.

The Cubs' current owners, the Ricketts family, began Project 1060 (named after the field's address) in 2014. A $750 million redevelopment, it added a 30,000-square-foot clubhouse, luxury corporate boxes, and a six-story administrative office building. Nearby is the Hotel Zachary (named after the field's architect), a shopping center, and an open-air plaza, Gallagher Way.

Wrigley Field was named a Chicago Landmark in 2004. It was named to the National Register of Historic Places in 2020.

Let's play ball!

4895 North Ravenswood Avenue

YANNELL NET-ZERO ENERGY RESIDENCE

2009: Farr Associates

Looking toward the future with an environmental eye, architect Doug Farr designed Chicago's first net-zero energy home, i.e., one that produces more energy (40 percent) than it consumes, on Chicago's North Side. While doing so, he also created an interesting campus for a house with two defined wings of different heights, one for living and one for sleeping, set in a landscape of native plants.

When it was built, it was dubbed the "Greenest House in America," with a platinum (the highest) LEED rating (Leadership in Energy and Environmental Design rating from the US Green Building Council). It was Illinois's first such certification.

Photovoltaic and solar thermal panels line the roofs, and because they are shaped like butterfly wings they are hidden from view. The V-shaped roofs also capture and propel rainwater downward. Their outsized shapes offer shade from the sun during the summer months, and their uneven heights increase southern exposure for the passive solar heating and allow for maximum cross-ventilation.

The photovoltaic panels generate most of the home's power needs, while the solar thermal panels create the heat for domestic water uses and radiant interior floors. The garage in the basement also is the location of the technology needed for the first gray-water system approved for a Chicago single-family house. Among other ways to save, spent water from the washing machine is collected and filtered back for use to flush toilets. Under the home is a geothermal heat exchange system.

Materials used to build the house were sustainable. For example, the oak flooring came from wood in the home that was previously on the site. Recycled newspapers became kitchen countertops.

The house "demonstrates that beautiful, sustainable, energy-positive housing can be integrated seamlessly into existing housing stock in northern climates," according to Farr Associates.

CHARLES M. HARPER CENTER

5807 South Woodlawn Avenue

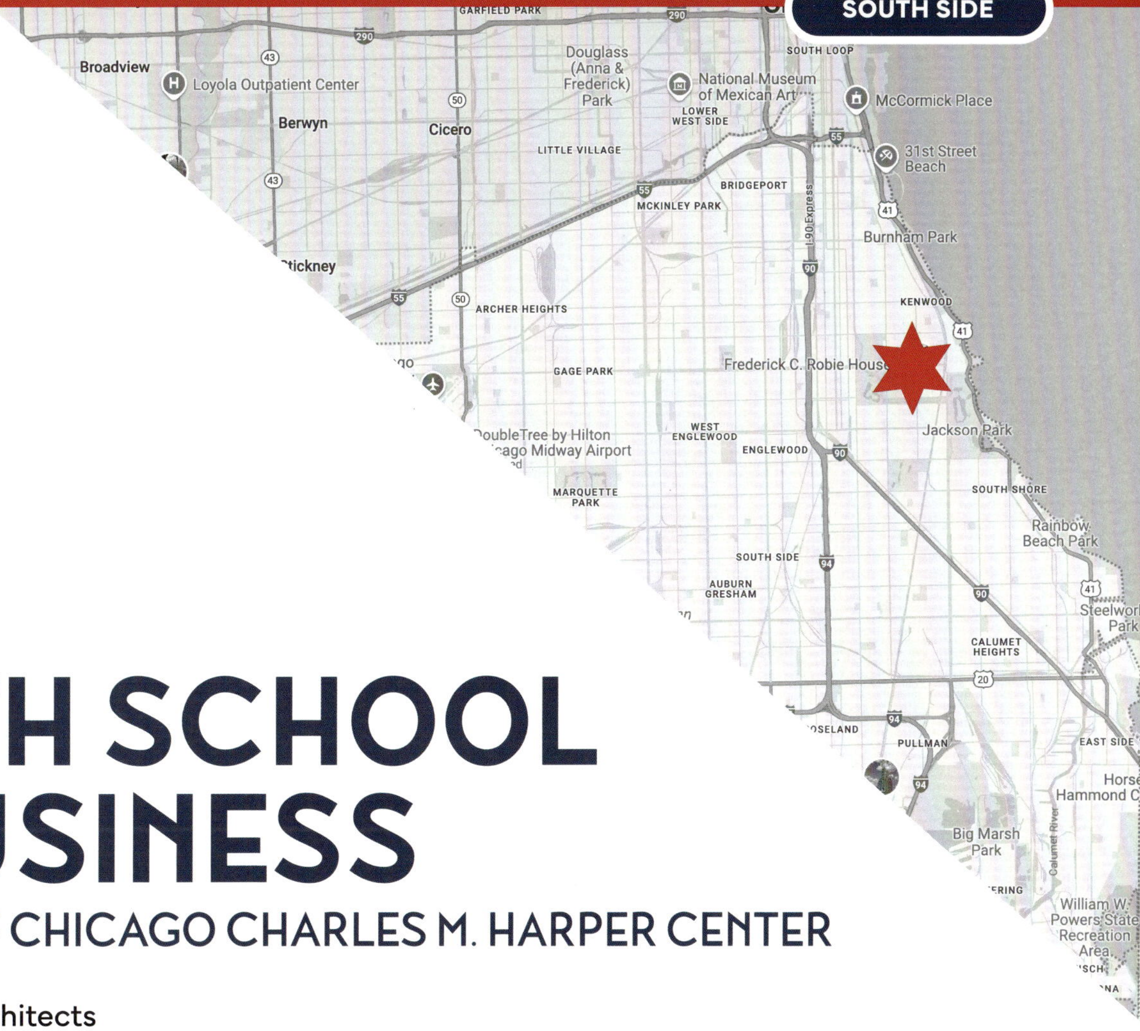

BOOTH SCHOOL OF BUSINESS

UNIVERSITY OF CHICAGO CHARLES M. HARPER CENTER

2004: Rafael Viñoly Architects

The Harper Center that houses the University of Chicago's Booth School of Business is a Post-Modern design paying homage to the adjacent Frank Lloyd Wright–designed Prairie-style Robie House as well as the collegiate Gothic-style Rockefeller Memorial Chapel, designed by Bertram Grosvenor Goodhue, across the street.

A spectacular building, it features cantilevered wings—sections that flare out with support from only one end—extending from the central Winter Garden that provides the building's focus. It is a large gathering space infused with natural light, down to the below-grade classrooms.

Architect Rafael Viñoly has completed many collegiate buildings on both this and other campuses, but this one stands out. The central Winter Garden is not only pleasing aesthetically but also, as is common on Post-Modern buildings, reminiscent of the past. Here the forms remind us first of the light wells incorporated in many of Chicago's early skyscrapers, such as the Rookery or the Monadnock, but also harkening to the soaring interior of nearby Rockefeller Chapel.

The Winter Garden's glass roof is held up by a set of four four-pointed vaults of tubular steel with proportions that follow those of the Rockefeller Chapel's lancet windows. The main structural columns flare outward as they rise, resembling the branches of trees in a garden. Their function is to funnel rainwater through the center of the columns into a reservoir.

The lower portion of the building perimeter is clad in horizontal panels of the same Indiana limestone that is widely used on other campus structures. Faculty offices above the base are clad with a glazed curtain wall.

The six-story building allowed the internationally renowned business school to consolidate its offices and classrooms previously located in at least six locations around campus. It stands out in its central campus location.

THROUGHOUT CHICAGO

CHICAGO BUNGALOW

1910s–1940s: Various architects

The Chicago Bungalow, a single-family home on its own parcel of land, was the answer to many housing problems of early 20th-century Chicago. It was decidedly an improvement over densely populated tenements, offering workers better living conditions and home ownership.

Bungalows proliferated from 1910 to the 1930s. Today, Chicago has more than 80,000 bungalows, one-third of the city's single-family housing stock. They occupy a wide, C-shaped swath fittingly called "The Bungalow Belt" that stretches from the northwest to southwest in a wide arc across the city's western edge. The Chicago Bungalow Association identifies 16 separate National Register Bungalow Historic Districts, areas where the homes, while perhaps not individually significant, are important as a collection.

Chicago Bungalows generally are one-and-a-half-story rectangular single-family, most of solid brick construction with face brick in the front and stone trim, topped by a low-pitched roof with wide overhangs. They feature banded or grouped windows, decorative brickwork, and limestone detailing. Bungalows boasted a full basement and the then-modern amenities of central heating, electricity, and indoor plumbing.

Bungalows often sit side by side, shaped somewhat by Chicago's long, narrow lots, usually 25 to 37 feet wide by 125 feet deep. While bungalows were affordable mainly due to their uniform designs, builders changed details such as color and entrance position to keep each home unique.

Entrances were small open-to-the air front porches. The remaining building front was enclosed in a bay, either rectangular or angled, and functioned as an extension of the living room. In the 1920s, art glass often was used in the bay windows.

The Bungalow Association offers more than 36 programs to help owners maintain and/or upgrade their homes.

Photo: The South Shore Bungalow Historic District, between East 75th and 78th Streets, and between Crandon and Clyde Avenues, contains 229 bungalows built between 1911 and 1930, among the city's first.

7723

O'HARE
150

3647 South State Street

CHICAGO PUBLIC LIBRARY, CHICAGO BEE BRANCH

(*CHICAGO BEE* BUILDING)

1929–31: Z. Erol Smith

This building's Art Deco designs are siren calls to come admire the lower level's gold and black panels, but also to look up to amazing panels in two shades of green terra-cotta. The three-story, nearly block-long structure's facade features spirals, nautilus forms, and organic shapes. This is not your typical Chicago Public Library.

The library is located in the former headquarters of the *Chicago Bee*, one of the many Black newspapers published for Chicago's African American community in the 1920s. The *Bee*, launched in 1926 by entrepreneur Anthony Overton, operated out of this building until it folded in the 1940s. Also on-site was the Overton Hygienic Cosmetics Co., which sold cosmetics aimed at African American customers. When that failed, the building was left empty, to be rescued later and restored by the city for library use.

The exterior terra-cotta (clay in a mold baked at high temperatures) was created by the Northwestern Terra Cotta Co. in Art Deco, the popular design style of the 1920s and '30s. It is characterized by sleek geometric and stylized forms. Some say the building's design was intended to reflect 1920s Black modernity and style. Architect Z. Erol Smith trained at the local Armour Institute of Technology (today's Illinois Tech). Much of his body of work is found on Chicago's South Side.

The *Chicago Bee* Building is one of nine landmarked structures in the federal Black Metropolis-Bronzeville Historic District, established in 2023. The area encompasses the story of the Great Migration, the exodus of millions of African Americans from the South to the North in the years 1916–1970, and highlights the commercial and artistic history of the Black neighborhood. Originally called Black Metropolis after a 1945 sociological study of the area, the neighborhood was later dubbed Bronzeville, a term attributed to a *Bee* editor.

2100 South Wentworth Avenue

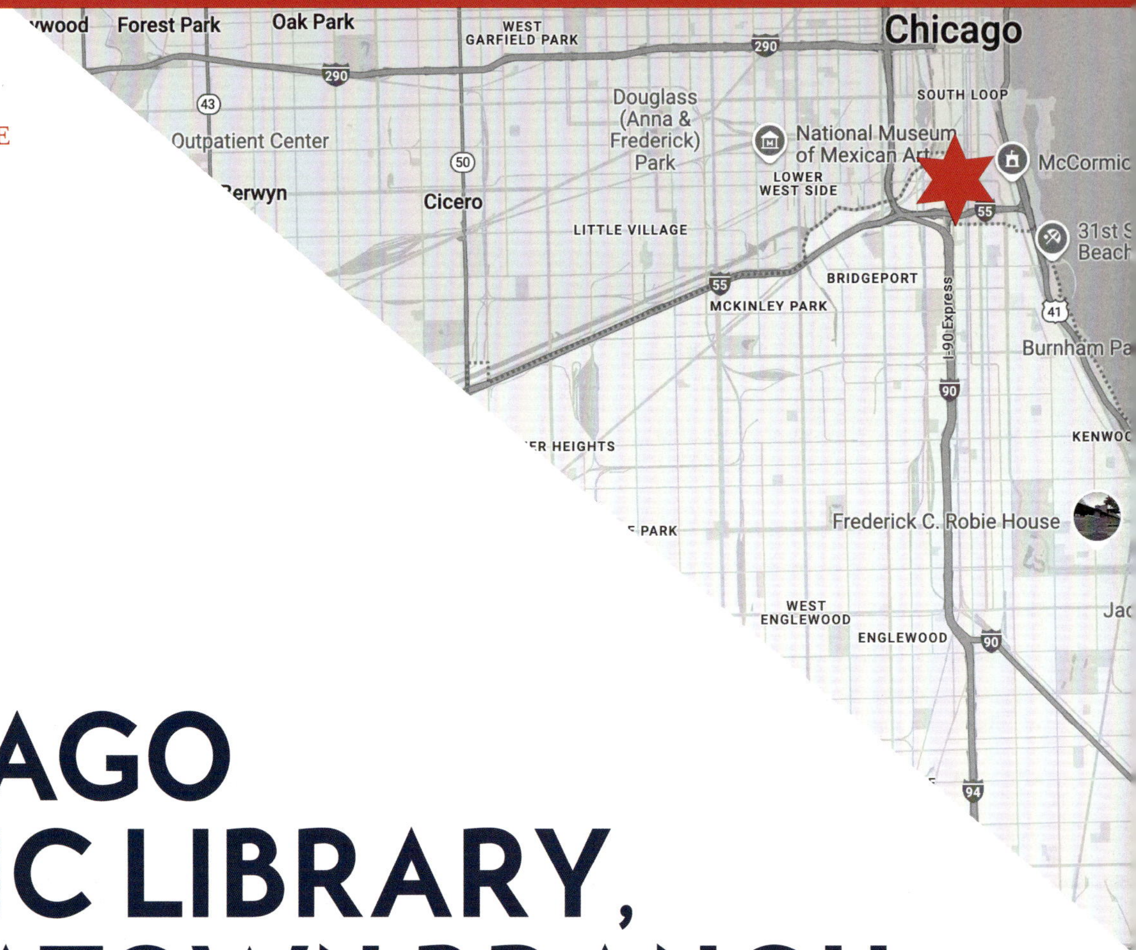

CHICAGO PUBLIC LIBRARY, CHINATOWN BRANCH

2015: Skidmore, Owings & Merrill, Brian Lee, project manager; Wight & Co., architect of record

This building's gently rounded triangular shape says loud and clear how it is unlike other, mostly architecturally bland, Chicago public libraries. The architecture style may be Modernist, but the design underpinnings come from the Chinese philosophy of feng shui.

Architect Brian Lee chose not to use literal Chinese architecture but instead to refer to the Chinese culture of screen facades and column-lined courtyards. The building is in harmony with the philosophy that balance in the natural world is needed to receive positive energy flow. The entrance appears slightly off-center, but it is placed there responding to feng shui.

A glass curtain wall around the building brings in natural light—and at night it glows like a Chinese lantern. Vertical metal fins are part of solar shading screens integrated into the curtain wall to reduce heat from the sun without blocking views to the outside. Like a traditional Chinese courtyard, all interior spaces connect to a central atrium, providing a clear orientation.

On the second floor, a 60-foot mural, *Universal Transverse Immigration Proclamation* by C.J. Hungerman, represents the past, present, and future of Chinatown. Hungerman calls his art Visual Riot—chaotic patterns, shapes, vibrant colors, and optic riddles. It is decidedly in contrast to a more traditional mosaic figurative mural, *Chinese in America* (1993) by Zhou Ping and Yan Dong, at the entrance to "new" Chinatown Square, 2154 South Archer Avenue, across the street.

The building functions as the link between the "old" Chinatown along Wentworth Avenue and the "new" Chinatown centered in Chinatown Square. It set the stage for new, innovative designs for Chicago's public libraries and operates as much as a community center for the neighborhood as it does a library, although it also has a large collection of volumes in Chinese.

PUBLIC
CHINATOWN
芝加哥公共图书馆华埠分馆
RETURNS

3360 SOUTH STATE STREET

S. R. CROWN HALL

(ARMOUR INSTITUTE, ILLINOIS INSTITUTE OF TECHNOLOGY COLLEGE OF ARCHITECTURE)

1956: Ludwig Mies van der Rohe; PACE Associates and C. F. Murphy Associates, associate architects

Although the campus of Illinois Tech (formerly Illinois Institute of Technology) is filled with almost two dozen Mid-Century Modernist buildings designed by master architect Ludwig Mies van der Rohe, Crown Hall is the crown jewel. It is an almost perfect expression of Miesian philosophy, using Modernist materials and proportion, with no applied ornamentation. The building and its proportions are optimal for architecture students and their classes.

A steel-and-glass walled pavilion, it is a singular space: 220 feet wide, 120 feet deep, and 28 feet high. The glass box appears to hover or float above the ground, its flat roof suspended from four huge I-beams that wrap around the building. Travertine steps, also seeming to float, mark the entrances.

Crown Hall is the home for Illinois Tech's School of Architecture. Mies headed the school after his arrival from Germany in 1938. He was the last dean of the Bauhaus school of modern art that was closed by the Nazi regime, which deemed the art and architecture "decadent."

When he arrived in the US, Mies was offered both the deanship and the opportunity to design the campus of the then-named Armour Institute. In all, he designed a campus of 20 buildings, most using the design element of "modules" or blocks for both the buildings and the spaces between them. Most campus buildings use steel, concrete, glass, or pale-yellow brick. With Crown Hall, Mies expanded space and jettisoned the module to create his masterpiece.

Called one of the 20th century's most important buildings, Crown Hall was named a Chicago Landmark in 1996, 10 years before it was officially eligible, and in 2001 was placed on the National Register of Historic Places and made a National Historic Landmark.

3137 SOUTH FEDERAL STREET

ED KAPLAN FAMILY INSTITUTE

FOR INNOVATION AND TECH ENTREPRENEURSHIP

2018: John Ronan Architects

The first new academic building in 40 years at Illinois Tech appears for all the world to be enveloped by pillows.

The campus at Illinois Tech, formerly the Illinois Institute of Technology, is filled with buildings designed by uber architect Ludwig Mies van der Rohe, constructed decades ago in the Mid-Century Modern style: dark metal and glass with no ornamentation. Architect John Ronan's Contemporary-style design has a similar underlying structure but adds state-of-the-art materials that substantially change the look of the building and significantly increase sustainability.

The upper floors, which are cantilevered over (extended beyond) the first, are clad in white ETFE foil cushions—or pillows. ETFE was developed in the aeronautics industry and later adopted by designers due to its energy efficiency. The foil, made of several layers separated by air chambers, automatically adjusts (inflates or deflates) to alter the amount of sunlight entering the building and reduce glare and energy use. It is the first use of ETFE in Chicago.

Built around two open-air courtyards, which allow air and light to penetrate at all levels, the building allows visitors to enter from various directions. As people enter the building they encounter "collision nodes," or spaces for chance meetings and information exchange.

The first floor is open, surrounded by glass walls, with a flow among state-of-the-art fabrication facilities, collaboration suites, and a bleacher-style stair that has become an informal seating area. Because the Kaplan Institute promotes collaboration, innovation, and entrepreneurship, the building includes a variety of collaboration spaces for university project-based experiences.

"It's an idea factory," Ronan has said, "a place of creative collision between students and faculty across disciplines, where new ideas are explored and tested on their way to becoming meaningful innovations." All in a building that itself is created with innovative sustainability ideas.

1800 South Prairie Avenue

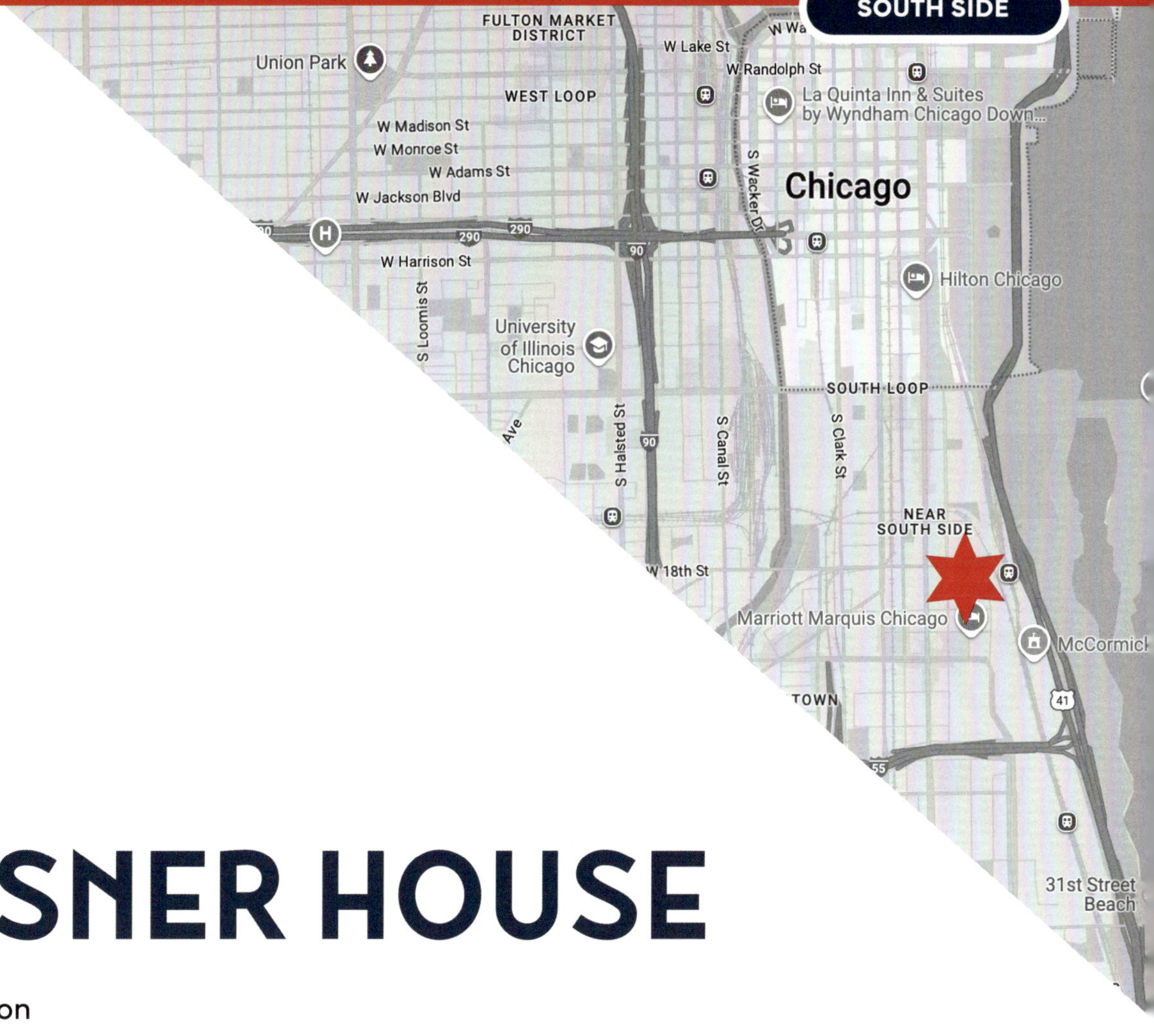

GLESSNER HOUSE

1886–7: H. H. Richardson

In the 1880s, a Chicago couple sought out Boston's nationally known—and some said America's greatest—architect, H. H. Richardson, to design their home on Prairie Avenue. In the process they brought to Chicago the best example of domestic design in the so-called Richardsonian Romanesque style.

John Glessner, executive for a firm that would become International Harvester, and his wife, Frances, hired Richardson based on his reputation. And they loved the house. However, the Glessners' neighbors were stunned. Prairie Avenue, the equivalent of today's Astor Street, where wealthy and famous industrialists lived, was not ready for this new look.

Looking for all the world like a fortress, Richardson's design protected its inhabitants from city noise and provided airy interiors and gracious living space—but none was visible from the street. Richardson's style modified French and Spanish Romanesque to American needs and broke totally with the Greek and Gothic styles fashionable at the time. Glessner House was a bold departure from the traditional Victorian architecture found around it.

Created of rough-hewn granite blocks, the front facade is stolid with few windows. Inside, the 17,000-square-foot house features family rooms that open onto an interior courtyard. The house was designed to accommodate the family—John, Frances, and their children—and a live-in staff of eight. Part of Chicago's upper-class society, Frances Glessner kept a journal recording visits from famous and interesting people who visited, creating a valuable history of the house and the times.

Today, the building is a house museum. It was one of Chicago's first Landmarks, designated in October 1970, and is a contributing building in the 1979 Prairie Avenue Historic District. It was entered on the National Register of Historic Places in April 1970 and elevated as a National Historic Landmark in December 1976.

5700 South DuSable Lake Shore Drive

GRIFFIN MUSEUM OF SCIENCE AND INDUSTRY

(ORIGINALLY PALACE OF FINE ARTS; MUSEUM OF SCIENCE AND INDUSTRY)

1893: D. H. Burnham & Co., Charles Atwood, architect
1929–40: Reconstruction: Graham, Anderson, Probst & White

A massive, impressive example of Beaux Arts style, this museum was originally built for the 1893 World's Columbian Exposition, used as the Palace of Fine Arts. It is the last fair building still standing on the site.

Following the Neo-Classical or Beaux Arts style, the building's facades resemble ancient Greek architecture: Corinthian columns, porticos, a Roman dome, and symmetrical design. The famous caryatids—statues of women holding up a porch roof—replicate 421 BC caryatids on Athens's Acropolis.

Fires in 1894 destroyed most fair buildings, but this still stands because it was an art museum. To protect the borrowed art the building was fire-proofed, built of brick with fire doors between galleries. To match the appearance of other buildings in the so-called White City, the bricks were covered in staff—plaster strengthened with horsehair and hemp—and painted white.

After the fair, the Columbian Museum, with collections left from the fair, opened in the building. Those were later moved to the new Field Museum of Natural History. The Palace of Fine Arts was left empty, rapidly deteriorating.

Philanthropist Julius Rosenwald helped fund the building's restoration and its reopening as an interactive science museum. Restoration meant the staff walls were stripped, the interior gutted to create open spaces for exhibits, and the exterior walls reclad in limestone, creating an exact replica of the original. The Museum of Science and Industry re-opened in time for the 1933 Century of Progress. Today, its massive size and sparkling white exterior are monuments to the 1893 fair.

During the fair, the building's main entrance faced south, opening out to a lagoon. Closed since fair's end, a $10 million renovation to reopen the entrance was announced in January 2025.

The building became a Chicago Landmark in November 1995.

2013 South Clark Street

HILLIARD TOWERS APARTMENTS

(HILLIARD HOMES)

1966: Bertrand Goldberg & Associates

Public housing is not usually considered anywhere near great. But architect Bertrand Goldberg designed public housing to provide a quality of life for Chicago Housing Authority residents equal to those who lived in his privately owned residential buildings, including Marina City. "I didn't design for the poor," he said. "I designed for the people."

Design-wise, this is Goldberg all the way, with curves and circles in a Mid-Century Modernist style that belies the rectangular glass and steel of its major advocate and Goldberg's former teacher, Ludwig Mies van der Rohe. Goldberg here—as in his other buildings—uses curves in flexible concrete because he said he resigned from "the right-angle club," instead following the dictum that there is no such thing as a right angle in nature.

Altogether, the 12.5-acre campus consists of four 22-story Brutalist-style towers with 654 housing units for low-income families and seniors. Brutalism is a style that is raw, rugged, and often imposing in appearance. It is defined by the prominent use of exposed concrete, emphasizing its texture and massiveness. The two round towers are for seniors, and the two crescent-shaped buildings to the north have living quarters for families. Goldberg believed the intermingling of generations was one key to good living.

Originally, the Hilliard Homes complex was a public housing project. Named in 1966 after Raymond M. Hilliard, director of the Cook County Department of Welfare, 1954–1966, the complex was recognized as a "model community, socially as well as architecturally." In 1999, under a redevelopment agreement, a private business assumed ownership and oversaw a $98 million complex rehabilitation. The buildings continue to cater to low-income renters.

The National Register of Historic Places in September 1999 listed the complex as part of the Raymond M. Hilliard Center Historic District.

3201 SOUTH STATE STREET

ILLINOIS TECH MCCORMICK TRIBUNE CAMPUS CENTER

2003: OMA (Office for Metropolitan Architecture), Rem Koolhaas, architect; with Studio Gang; Holabird & Root, associate architects

It is not often that a building has a train running on top of it, but this one does: An oval tube of concrete clad in corrugated steel sits on the roof to accommodate the Green Line "L" that runs through about every 15 minutes. The acoustical tunnel's job is to buffer the sound.

The building, whose design was selected following an international competition, is the crossroad of a campus filled with Ludwig Mies van der Rohe-designed classroom buildings, Mid-Century Modernism in all its glory: glass-and-steel structures, regulation along a grid, and a similarity of look. But this, the first building on the Illinois Tech (formerly Illinois Institute of Technology) campus since 1971, is bold and different: it deals directly with the "L"; it features a diagonal composition with two lines of travel within the building crossing paths, turning the building into an urban intersection; and it incorporates Commons Hall, a Mies-designed building, to boot.

It is a complex, busy design for a busy one-story building housing the usual student union space requirements in its 100,000 square feet: snack stops, a game area, a convenience store, study areas, and a bookstore. Colors are used to delineate specific areas, with orange on one wall, green and red on others.

The building functions as the informal intersection between Illinois Tech's western campus academic buildings and its eastern residence halls.

On the exterior, industrial materials such as steel and glass were used, much like Modernism, but the design becomes Post-Modern not only with its unusual shape and rooftop train tunnel, but also with its playful portrait of Mies in glass on the entry doors on the west side. Does it seem he is smiling at this wow! building integrated into "his" campus? Who knows? Maybe.

Emergency

1100 EAST 57TH STREET

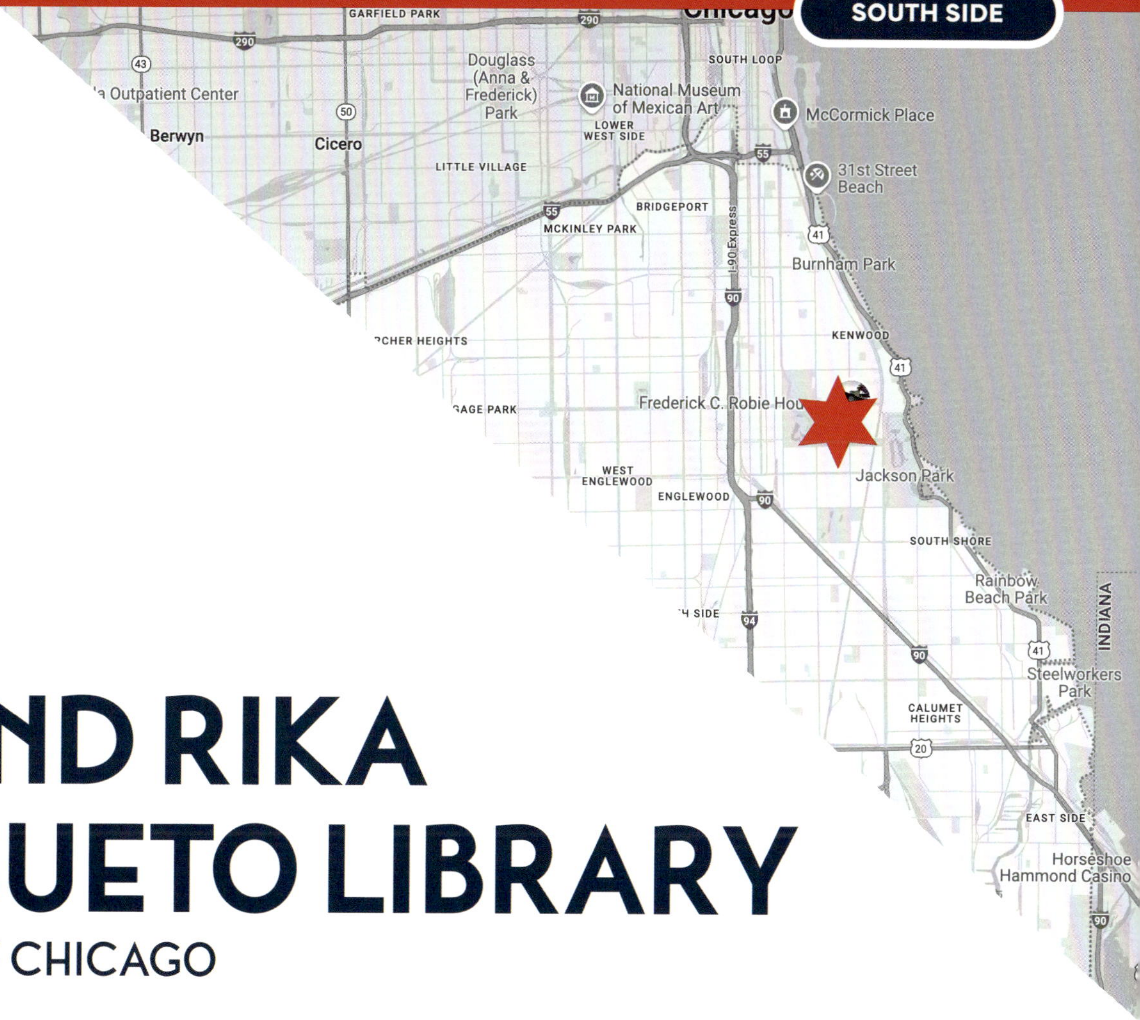

JOE AND RIKA MANSUETO LIBRARY

UNIVERSITY OF CHICAGO

2012: Murphy/Jahn

Only the egg-shaped glass top of this university library is visible from the street. Yet the effect is very futuristic—and bespeaks a break in tradition.

The buried building is the solution to the problem of a small lot for a large job—storing 3.5 million-plus volumes the university library owns, space for preservation laboratories, and a reading room. All this on a site that is only 160 feet by 360 feet. In the design, books are deployed 55 feet below ground, where environmental controls provide constant temperatures and humidity. Robotic cranes find and retrieve books for readers within five minutes.

The public spaces, such as the reading room, are located at ground level under the dome that rises 35 feet at its center. Preservation, conservation, and digitization labs share the first level with the grand-scale reading room. Architect Helmut Jahn used crisscrossing steel curved beams to carry the weight of the glass panels in the soaring elliptical dome. The panels have fritted glass, meaning a pattern is applied to the glass, which filters out ultraviolet rays and solar heat. It also keeps birds from flying into the structure.

Architecture critic Blair Kamin jokingly called the building the Book Bubble, the Dome for Tomes, or the Spaceship that Made Reading Oh-So-Cool, speculating that a sci-fi movie will soon seek to use the location. It's easy to see why, with its uniquely 21st-century shape.

Mansueto's 21st-century library is connected to its neighbor, the 1970s Brutalist-style Regenstein Library, by glass walkways. Both libraries feature underground facilities, but are very different. Yet, on the ground level, the limestone and rugged look of the Brutalist building complements the smooth, silky glass look of Mansueto's Contemporary style.

The library's northern neighbor is Henry Moore's *Nuclear Energy* sculpture, identifying the site of the first self-sustaining, controlled nuclear chain reaction.

350 East Cermak Road

LAKESIDE TECHNOLOGY CENTER

(R. R. DONNELLEY & SONS CALUMET PLANT)

1912–24: Howard Van Doren Shaw
1929: west-central, south sections, including tower: Charles Z. Klauder

Lakeside is one of the city's—perhaps the nation's—finest essays in industrial Gothic, according to the American Institute of Architects Chicago guidebook. This 1.2-million-square-foot building stands out for its exterior design and ornamentation, more than holding its own in what today is a busy convention-oriented location, near the McCormick Place Convention Center.

Originally a facility for R. R. Donnelley, the printer of the telephone directories of the pre–cell phone age as well as the humongous Sears catalogs, the huge concrete building was transformed into the Midwest's largest data center and one of the largest in the world in 1999.

When the building was constructed, Donnelley's chief exec, Thomas E. Donnelley, sought "to make the whole building dignified and beautiful—something that will be beautiful not only today, but 100 years from now." How prescient he was.

For its exterior, architect Howard Van Doren Shaw chose a variety of materials: limestone arches over the windows, stone medallions, terra-cotta plaques and seals. The wall piers provide vertical support, stepping out like buttresses, between the set-back windows. Medallions and plaques depict stylized marks and devices of early printers such as Johannes Gutenberg.

At the main entry are six seals, three with the initials of the architect and owners, and carved relief panels showing a Native American on one facing a frontier pioneer on the other.

The building was built in segments and finished in 1929. The last section, the tall tower, designed by collegiate designer Charles Klauder, formerly contained a two-story Gothic library.

The building was listed on the National Register of Historic Places in February 1983 and waited until March 2004 to be declared a Chicago Landmark.

REX

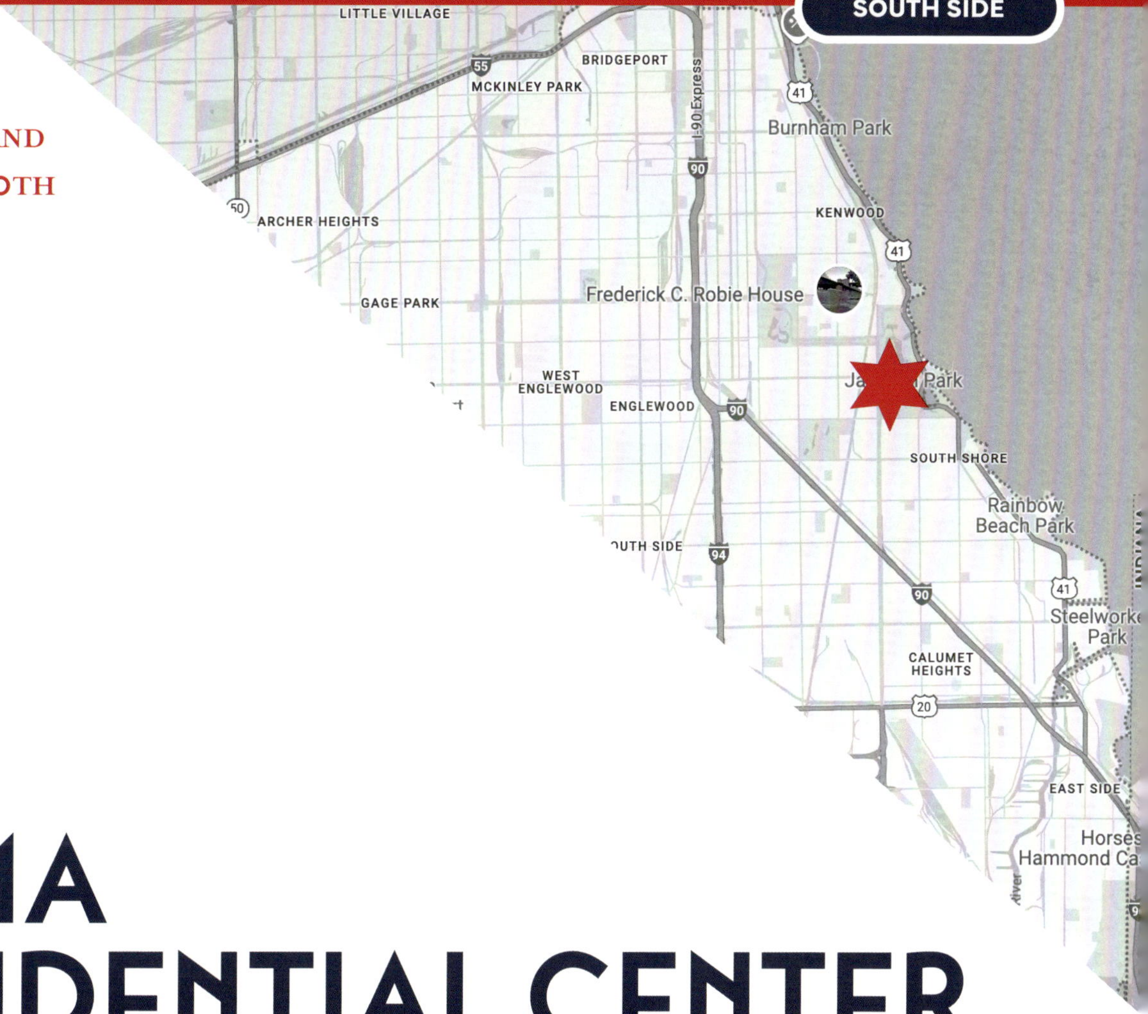

Jackson Park: East of Stony Island Avenue between 60th and 63rd Streets

OBAMA PRESIDENTIAL CENTER

2026 (projected): Tod Williams Billie Tsien Architects, Interactive Design Architects (IDEA)

It is difficult to critique a building that has not been completed, but the emergence of the almost-complete tower in Jackson Park that will become the Obama Presidential Center is so close to completion it cries out for inclusion.

The Contemporary-style main building, a 235-foot tower clad in stone, will be the main focus of a campus that includes a Modernist-looking gymnasium building, a sunken or below-ground Chicago Public Library, a plaza, and a park area that includes a sledding hill. The center constitutes a museum; it will not hold the archives of the Barack Obama presidency. Instead, it will function as a high-level community center.

Plans for a presidential center began in 2017 but, due to the location selected, in a public park designed in 1893 by renowned landscape architect Frederick Law Olmsted, groundbreaking waited until multiple lawsuits were adjudicated. Construction for the tower and road reconfiguration began in 2021. Dates for completion keep getting pushed out further.

Well-known landscape architect Michael Van Valkenburgh, working with Chicago-based Site Design Group, will landscape the 19-acre park and the roofs of the lower buildings to blend the project into the park. All the buildings will be connected below grade and "clad in a lively, warm, and variegated stone," according to the Obama Foundation.

The museum, the tallest of the three buildings, has stained-glass window inclusions on the north side and carved lettering on the top that repeats words from a 2015 Obama speech emphasizing the meaning of "we" in America.

Presidential libraries and centers aspire to the designation "greatest" as an honor for their presidents. This tower is meant to be a beacon to the city and aspires to that greatness. Whether it fulfills the mission has yet to be determined.

培德中心
PUI TAK CENTER

2216 SOUTH WENTWORTH AVENUE

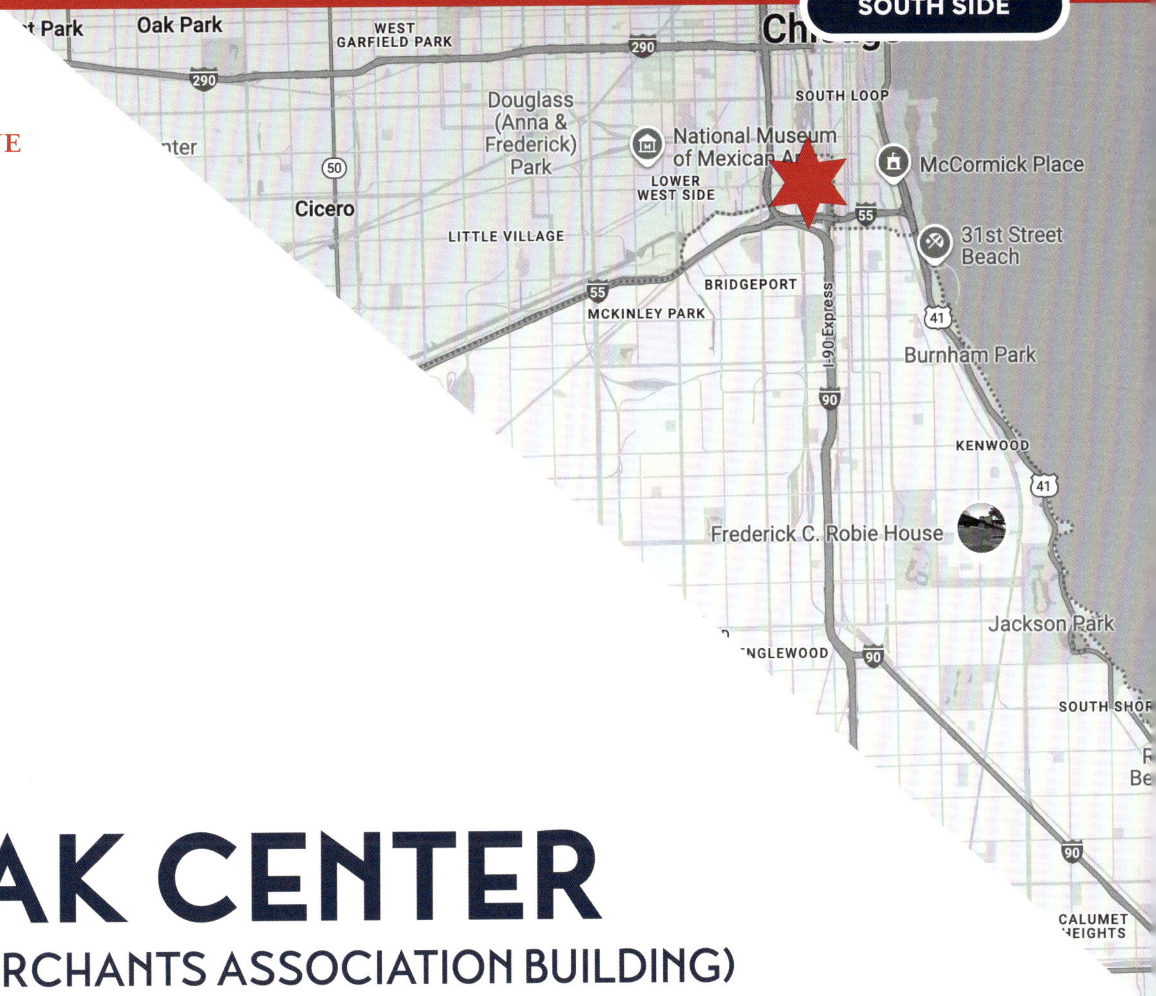

PUI TAK CENTER

(ON LEONG MERCHANTS ASSOCIATION BUILDING)

1928: Michaelsen & Rognstad

This, the *de facto* Chinatown City Hall, is a vision of Chinese architecture seen through the lens of Western architects.

Designed by two Americans because there were no registered Chinese architects in the city at the time, the building was headquarters for the On Leong (Chinese) Merchants Association, the equivalent of a chamber of commerce for the business district that had developed around Wentworth Avenue and Cermak Road. The merchants association wanted the building to reflect traditional Chinese architecture, to express pride in Chicago's Chinatown.

The building was described as "one of the most expensive and elaborate buildings ever erected in America by the Chinese," according to the *Chicago Tribune* at the time.

Rounded green clay roof tiles, overhanging eaves, together with pagodas (tiered towers with multiple eaves, one at each end of the building), are teamed with colorful terra-cotta tiles. These were American-made, by Teco Pottery in Crystal Lake, Illinois, and designed by the architects. They sport geometric patterns that represent good fortune and long life. In homeland China, tiles would not have been made of terra-cotta, clay that has been fired in hot temperatures for at least two days, but of glazed ceramic. Visually, however, the look was similar: a bit of homeland China along Wentworth Avenue.

On Leong meant a tong, one of a number of family groups that provided services to the community. But tongs also were often associated with illegal activities. In a 1988 raid of the building, the Federal Bureau of Investigation confiscated illegal gambling paraphernalia. After a trial and racketeering convictions, the feds took over. In 1993, the Chinese Christian Union Church bought the building and renamed it Pui Tak, or "cultivating virtue center." Today, it functions as a community center.

In 1993 Pui Tak Center was named a Chicago Landmark.

11001 South Cottage Grove Avenue

PULLMAN FACTORY AND ADMINISTRATION BUILDING

1880: Solon Beman

The factory and administration building is at the center of the Pullman District, a historic Chicago neighborhood and, since 2015, a National Monument showcasing late-19th-century industrial America. Architect Solon Beman designed the building, also called the Clock Tower and Administrative Center, and to boot, the entire town, often listed as one of the US's most beautiful industrial landscapes.

George Pullman, founder and owner of the highly successful Pullman Palace Car Co., created this planned community for workers at his railroad company. It was one of the US's first model planned industrial communities.

Brick homes were a luxury for most 19th-century workers. But in Pullman, everyone lived in a brick home—from the larger row houses near the factory set aside for company managers to the smaller workers' cottage row houses farther away. Distinctive red brick with white terra-cotta accents was used for all.

Other Beman-designed buildings on the site include the Hotel Florence, 11111 South Forrestville Avenue; the Greenstone Church, 11211 South St. Lawrence Avenue, named after its Pennsylvania green limestone color; and the homes located between 103rd and 115th Avenues, South Cottage Grove and South Ellis Street.

Pullman railroad workers struck in 1894 when the company cut wages but at the same time refused to reduce Pullman rents. In 1898, the Illinois Supreme Court forced the company to sell off the residential areas of Pullman as part of the strike settlement. Chicago annexed Pullman in 1889.

A visit to the Pullman site highlights wonderful architecture but also tells the history of social and economic forces that shaped modern America.

The state purchased the administration building in 1991 to create the Illinois Pullman State Historic Site. President Barack Obama designated the Pullman National Historical Park in 2015.

5757 South Woodlawn Avenue

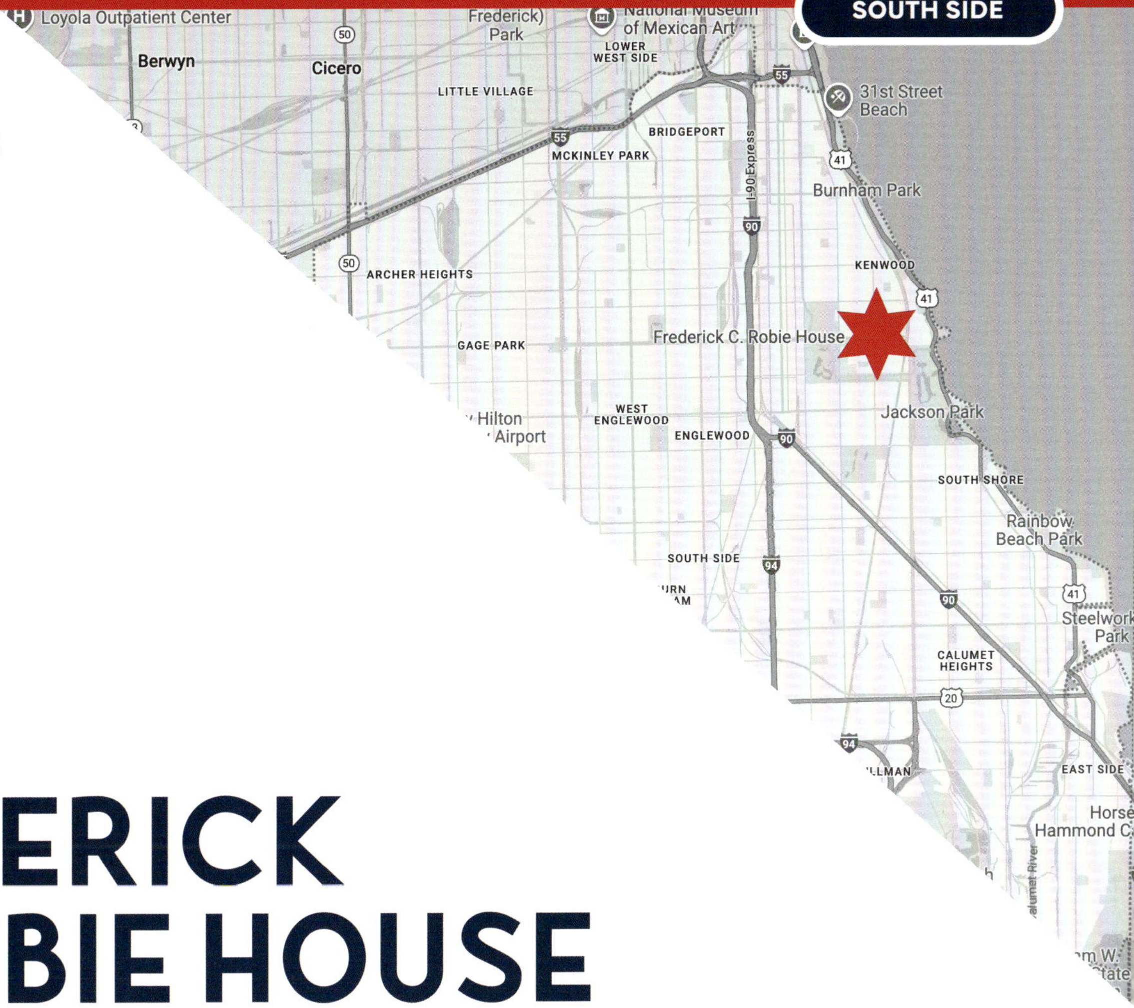

FREDERICK C. ROBIE HOUSE

1910: Frank Lloyd Wright
2019: Restoration: Harboe Architects

The front, thrusting forward like the prow of a ship, is akin to the face that launched 1,000 ships. This ship-like structure launched thousands of new-style residences that populated America throughout the 20th century.

Frank Lloyd Wright's Robie House is the exemplar of a Prairie-style house: brick, here Roman (thin) brick that emphasizes horizontality, with linear limestone trim; a hidden entrance forcing visitors through a tight access en route to the glorious openness of a living-dining area; art glass casement ribboned windows that catch the light—and so much more.

The building was a radical departure from what had come before—three- and even four-story Victorian homes, emphasizing verticality, with small, tightly defined rooms. Designed for bicycle and automobile supplies manufacturer Frederick C. Robie, it is one of the county's most famous residential structures.

Wright, who broke the pattern of residential living in the early 20th century, illustrated almost all of his stylistic highpoints here. Two two-story areas, one for bedrooms and one for the living-dining room, are capped by a smaller third floor. A large chimney tops it and allows for the double-sided fireplace central to the open interior space. The south-facing window wall provides privacy but blurs the limits between inside and out. Huge roof overhangs provide useable porches.

The Robies divorced two years after they moved in, at the same time Robie's business failed. The house passed into the hands of many different owners, most of whom did not honor its architectural legacy. Today, the house is owned by the Frank Lloyd Wright Trust, which restored the interior and exterior to their 1909 beginnings.

The house was designated a National Historic Landmark in 1963, entered the National Register of Historic Places in 1966, and became a Chicago Landmark in September 1971.

47TH STREET
AT MICHIGAN AVENUE

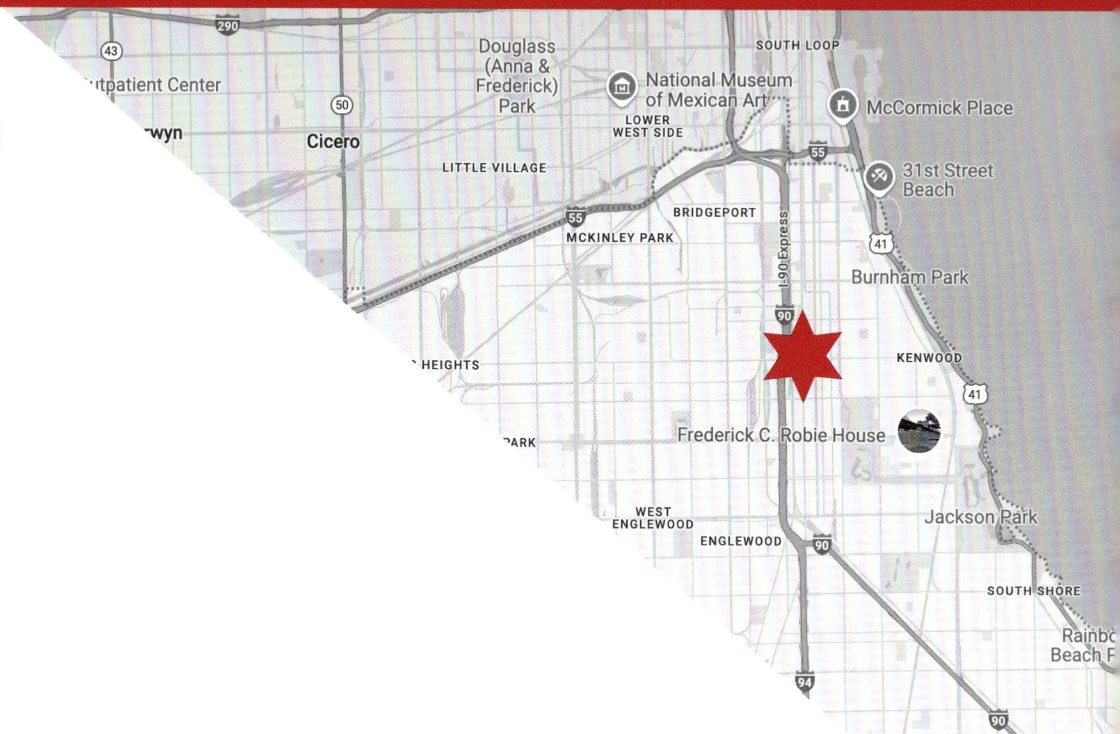

ROSENWALD COURTS

(ROSENWALD APARTMENTS; ORIGINALLY MICHIGAN BOULEVARD GARDEN APARTMENTS)

1929: Ernest Grunsfeld Jr.

In the era when Chicago was growing in population faster than any other city in the US, an apartment building occupying nearly a full city block was built around an interior courtyard. The Art Deco–style housing complex was built by Sears, Roebuck & Co. president Julius Rosenwald, who called it the Michigan Boulevard Garden Apartments. The building's early life was providing quality housing for Black residents who were prevented from moving out of the Bronzeville neighborhood due to discriminatory practices.

Rosenwald was one of the city's most noted philanthropists who supported many projects to improve the lot of Black people, including the famed Rosenwald Schools across the South. He was inspired by municipal subsidized housing he had seen in Vienna. Originally built as nongovernmental subsidized housing, the building is considered to be among the earliest mixed-use housing developments.

Architect Ernest Grunsfeld Jr., who was also Rosenwald's nephew, designed using colors—creamy tan brick contrasted with darker red-brown stripes—to create outside images for the 420 apartments with shops running along the ground floor facing 47th Street. The building was a haven for middle-class African Americans. But its profit margins were thin and following Rosenwald's death, the family withdrew. Disrepair and declining maintenance followed.

The building was turned over to the Chicago Housing Authority in 1974, and the poorly kept property was vacated in 2000. It then languished with loud lamenting but little action until a $132 million project restored the apartments in 2016. The building's apartment count was lowered to 239, and it was reconfigured with mostly affordable one- and two-bedroom units. Elevators and air-conditioning were added, and the interior courtyard was landscaped.

The building was added to the National Register of Historic Places in August 1981. In 2017, the city council approved it as a Chicago Landmark.

7059 South South Shore Drive

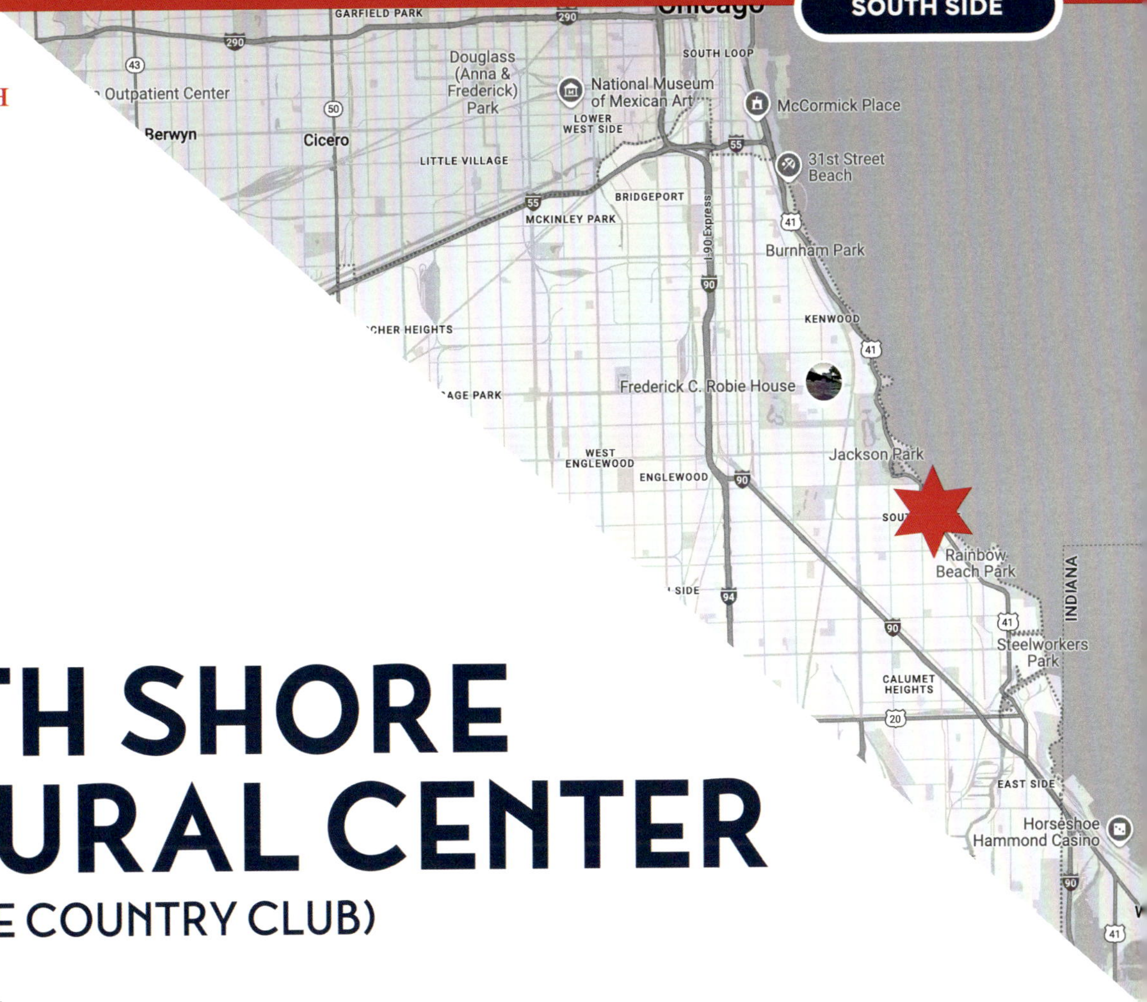

SOUTH SHORE CULTURAL CENTER

(SOUTH SHORE COUNTRY CLUB)

1916: Marshall and Fox
1983: Renovation: Norman DeHaan Associates

A grand example of grand living in the early 20th century, this clubhouse was part of a restricted country club for Chicagoans wealthy and famous. It has been transformed into a cultural community center open to everyone regardless of wealth, race, or religion.

The South Shore Country Club, founded in 1905, first hired architects Benjamin Marshall and Charles Fox, later known for their luxury hotel and apartment building designs including the Drake Hotel, to create a modest clubhouse. The club, on 65 acres including a golf course, tennis courts, and beach, quickly expanded; a larger, more substantial clubhouse was needed.

Constructed in 1916, this palatial building, again designed by Marshall and Fox, is made of reinforced concrete clad in stucco, designed in the Mediterranean Revival style, one rarely seen in Chicago but popular in warmer climates. The beautiful first-floor interiors include a ballroom, solarium, and dining room arranged around a grandly scaled, two-story-high passagio, or circulation foyer. Large ballrooms on each end and their connecting hallway are lavishly ornamented with finely detailed plaster details. The North Ballroom and its decorative ceiling have been likened to a glass box with a Wedgwood lid. Wall-to-wall windows open to a terrace overlooking the lake. Driving up to the clubhouse anticipates the magnificent architecture with a colonnaded entryway.

Club membership peaked in the 1950s, but it closed in the 1970s. In 1974, the Chicago Park District purchased the property to expand its lakefront properties, thinking to raze the deteriorating clubhouse. But community members rallied to save the building, pushing for rehabilitation into a culture center. Today, the park district has also restored the entry gate and stables (used by the Chicago Mounted Patrol Unit) at this, one of the most visually distinctive park buildings in the city.

800 West
Fulton Market

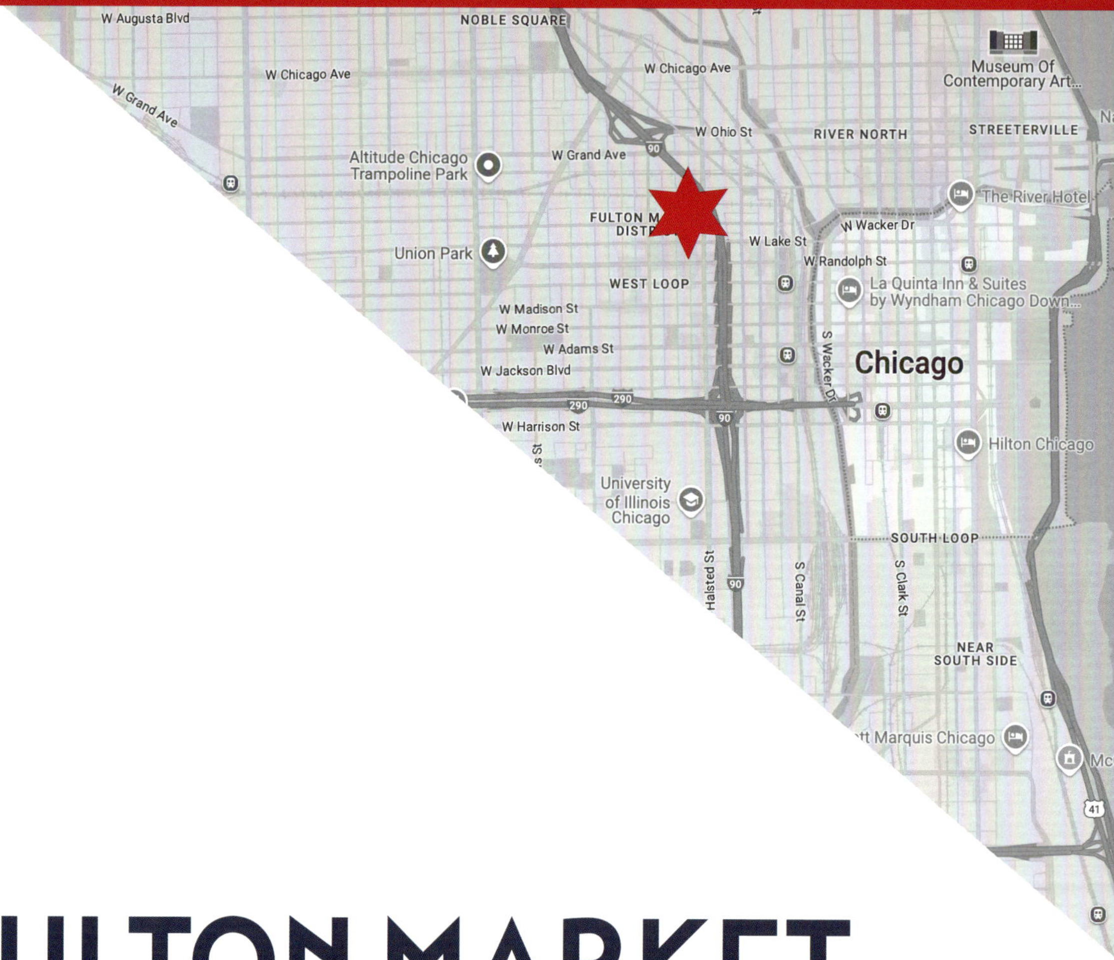

800 FULTON MARKET

2021: Skidmore, Owings & Merrill

Abutting the Fulton Market district, the "hottest" area in the city at the moment with a plethora of residential and office towers either already built or going up, 800 Fulton Market makes a statement of strength, with a tip of its hat to Chicago's industrial past.

Fulton Market was, originally, a meatpacking market area. It only recently has been developed as a prime hive of restaurants and boutique shopping amid new residential high-rises. Eight hundred is a 19-story building, set right across the street from the Fulton Market historic district, allowing it to have contemporary height yet still fit into the market scene with its brick and steel materials, terraces filled with native plantings, and visible front-facing cross-bracing steel.

The building is defined by its X-braced facades, harkening back to the John Hancock Building. External steel-braced frames on the east and west sides are engineered with Chicago's harsh, freeze-thaw winters in mind. The braces move closer or farther from the facade depending on the temperature, in a range of approximately nine inches. They also resist the wind. Together with offset cantilevers—floors reaching out with support only at one end—made of glass, the structural system enables large, open floor plates and flexible workspaces.

The mixed-use building touts its up-to-date modern technology: the nation's highest standard for commercial office indoor air quality with fresh air intake on each floor; abundant green spaces; and common outdoor decks.

Over 50 percent of the roof space is a green roof. That has resulted in a WELL Gold rating from the International WELL Building Institute. Its LEED (Leadership in Energy and Environmental Design) Platinum certification, the highest possible from the US Green Building Council, indicates sustainability. And, as only a contemporary building can, it gained Wired- and Smart-Scores, certifications in digital capability.

JOHN DEERE
COSTERA

300 North Central Park Avenue

GARFIELD PARK CONSERVATORY

1906–7: Jens Jensen and Schmidt, Garden & Martin; Hitchings & Co., engineers

Jens Jensen, a Scandinavian immigrant who espoused groundbreaking architectural landscaping ideas steeped in the Midwestern prairie, broke with convention with this building. Considered revolutionary when it opened, the conservatory is shaped like Illinois's prairie haystacks. Plants displayed from around the world are "rooted" here in both senses of the word: actually planted in Midwestern soil—there is no floor beneath the plant beds in the Palm House—and located in a building designed in the Midwestern Prairie style.

"We did not want our greenhouses to look like a palace, a château, or a Renaissance villa, but like a glass house for the cultivation of plants which everyone might enjoy," Jensen said, quoted on a Conservatory plaque. "In order to fit them into a prairie landscape I thought they might well take the outlines of the great haystacks which are so eloquent of the richness of prairie soil."

Today, the conservatory is one of the US's largest botanical conservatories, offering "landscape art under glass" in eight indoor display gardens plus 10 acres of outdoor gardens, nature play areas, and a water lily pond.

The conservatory replaced a group of smaller greenhouses in various parks, when Jensen took the reins as superintendent of the West Park Commission in 1905. Unlike the Victorian-era conservatories, which featured plants in pots, Jensen created open rooms and planted into the ground. He used stratified stone to separate the rooms and hide mechanical systems. In the Fern Room, the central room around which the others revolve, you find both a prairie waterfall and a pool bordered in stone.

Heat, humidity, and flowering plant scents hit you when you enter; they make visiting the conservatory a pleasure no matter the season.

The Garfield Park Conservatory was listed on the National Register of Historic Places in August 1993.

1835 West Harrison Street

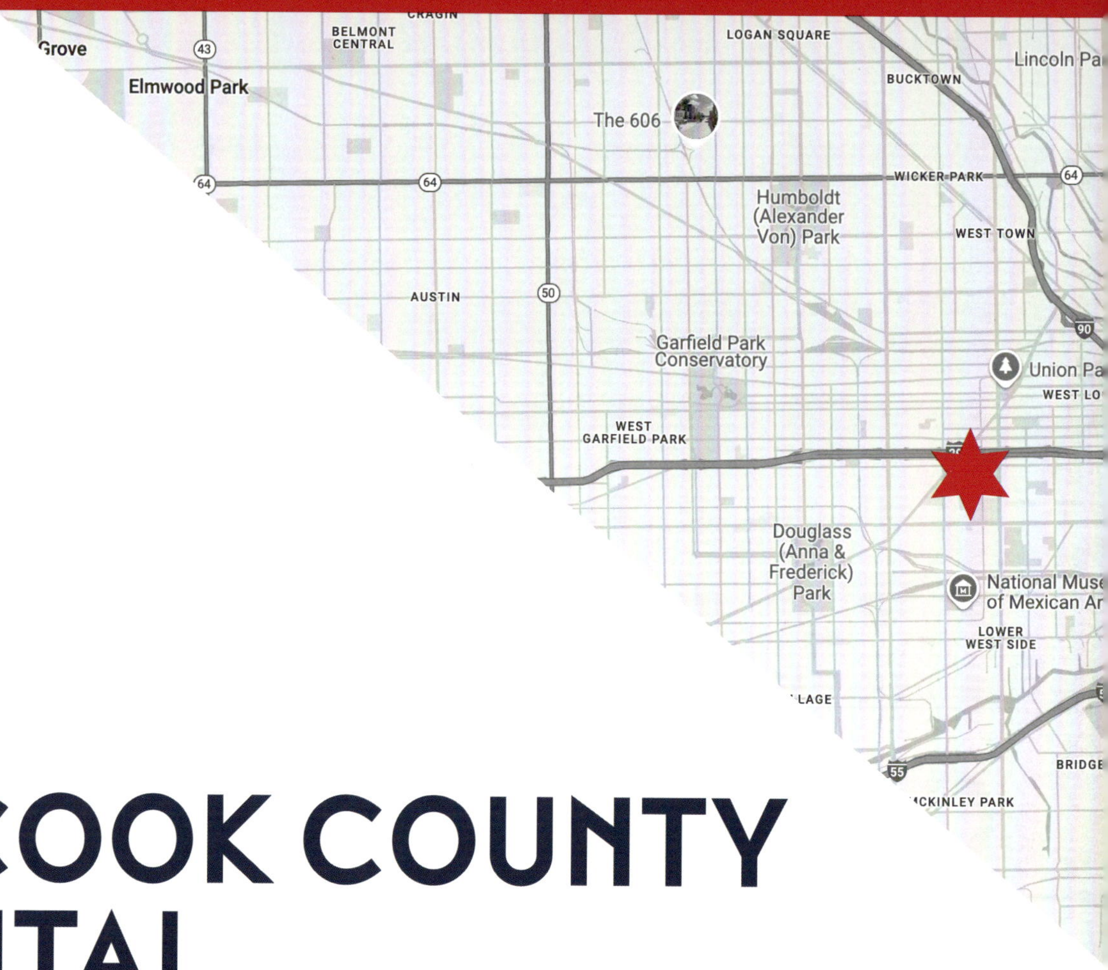

OLD COOK COUNTY HOSPITAL

1913: Paul Gerhardt
2020–21: Conversion: Skidmore, Owings & Merrill, KOO Architects

Snatched from the jaws of demolition as it literally was falling apart from lack of maintenance, Chicago's Cook County Hospital has not only been saved, but the massive, block-long magnificently ornamented Beaux Arts–style structure has been turned into a modern medical office building with two Hyatt hotels and a humongous food court.

The monumental—345,000-square-foot—hospital served immigrants, whether from Europe or the American South, for more than eight decades. During the 1920s, when African Americans moved north, the hospital was one of the few that did not discriminate. By the mid-20th century, 60 percent of all African American babies born in Cook County were delivered here.

In 1998, when ground was broken for a new $550 million hospital, the county planned to raze the old one by 2003 and replace it with a park. Preservationists, led by Landmarks Illinois and Preservation Chicago, mounted a two-decades-long campaign that changed the county board's mind—opting for restoration over demolition. On the building's facade alone, more than 4,160 individual pieces of terra-cotta were repaired or duplicated by Gladding McBean—one of only two US terra-cotta manufacturers.

Cook County Hospital was home to many medical firsts: the US's first blood bank, in 1937; first medical internship program; and first identification of sickle-cell anemia in the US. It also pioneered hiring the first female medical director and first female head of surgery for a major US hospital.

The hospital is "one of Chicago's grandest public buildings," says the City of Chicago Landmarks report, approved January 2019. The National Register of Historic Places designation, in 2006, added that the building may be unique in the nation—a monumental Beaux Arts structure built as a public charity hospital.

HYATT PLACE
HYATT house

4830 South
Western Avenue

CHICAGO PARK DISTRICT HEADQUARTERS

2023: John Ronan Architects

Looking at it head-on, the Chicago Park District's Headquarters Building, shared with the Brighton Park Community Campus, is two half-circles of what look like short silos facing one another.

The silo image is impressive, bringing back memories not only of farmland structures but also of Chicago's original skyscrapers: grain elevators. Yet, this building is also obviously new, reflecting its Contemporary style with energy-saving modern materials that have been reclaimed and reused, and a landscape that features native plants.

After long residencies in downtown Chicago offices, the move of the Park District headquarters to Brighton Park was partially a result of the INVEST South/West program of former mayor Lori Lightfoot, an effort using public funds to create buildings and new businesses in underserved communities; they then act as catalysts for more development.

The circular, 80,000-square-foot building is only two stories high, to respect its residential neighborhood, despite being located on formerly industrial land. A pathway through the building separates the field house/local park from the headquarters. The pathway is reminiscent of landscape architect Frederick Law Olmsted's creation of the Chicago boulevard system, where larger parks are connected via landscaped thoroughfares. Two open-air courtyards are in the center of the circle to bring in light and air and create an outdoor meeting space.

Chicago common brick, salvaged from nearby demolished buildings, is used decoratively at the front entry and along the passageways. The perimeter is bronze-tinted glass and curved metal screens in champagne-anodized aluminum (painted metal to prevent rust). The latter provides sun shade to improve energy efficiency as well as gives the building its distinctive appearance.

A green roof tops the structure, mitigating the urban "heat island" effect. Inside, ash wood reclaimed from local trees decimated by the emerald ash borer is used in furniture, wall cladding, and gym flooring.

18th Street and Canalport Avenue

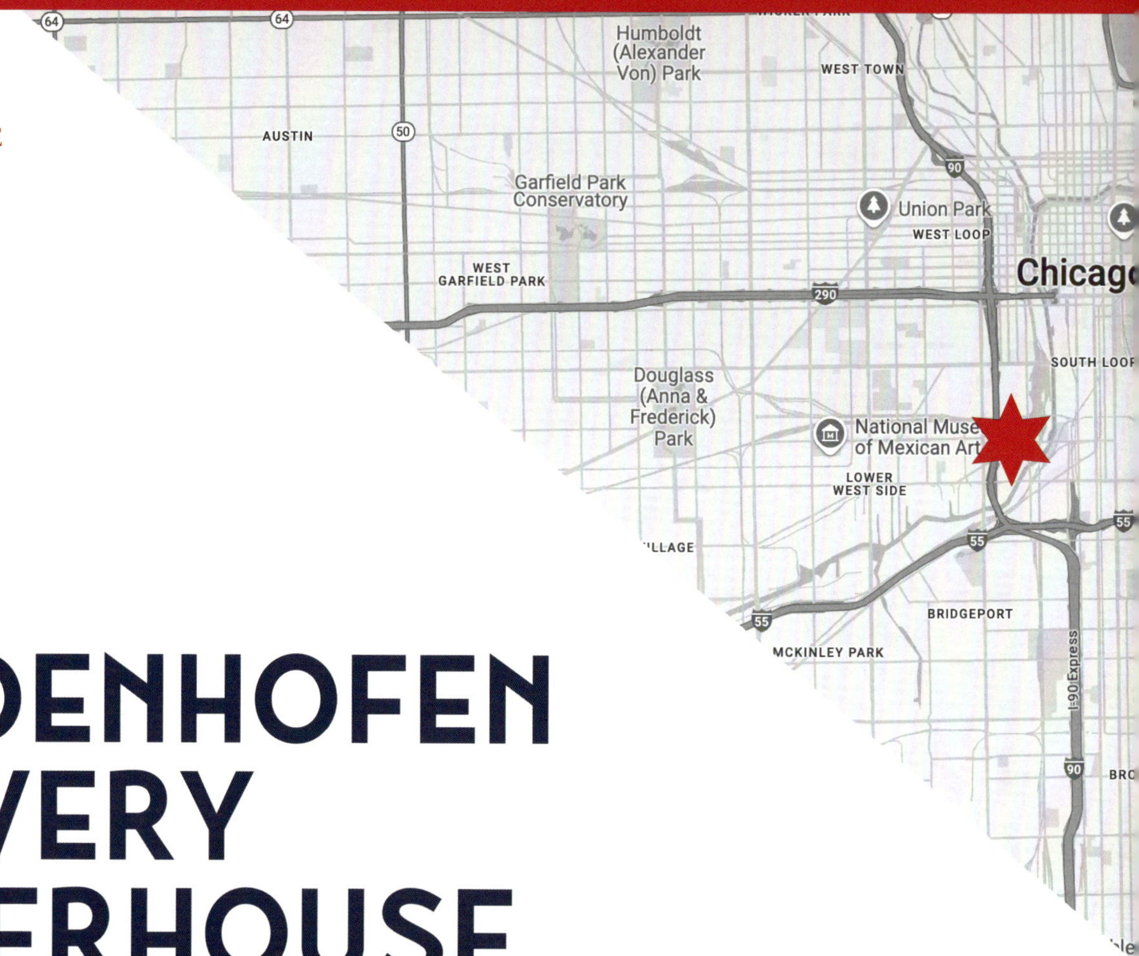

SCHOENHOFEN BREWERY POWERHOUSE

1902: Schmidt, Garden & Martin

This Prairie-style building is one of the last major pre-Prohibition brewery buildings still standing in Chicago. It illustrates both the city's industrial heritage and the mix of progressive architecture with manufacturing.

Brewing beer was a major part of Chicago's industrial base at the turn of the 20th century. Peter Schoenhofen Brewing Co. was established in 1861 by Peter Schoenhofen and Matheus Gottfried in the Pilsen (West Side) neighborhood. In 1867, Schoenhofen bought his partner out, moved production from its original location at Jefferson and 12th Streets to a newer facility at 18th Street and Canalport Avenue, and renamed the firm eponymously. By 1910, the brewery was producing more than 1.2 million barrels per year, Edelweiss its most popular brand.

Most of the original 15 buildings in what was a seven-acre complex are gone, including a machine shop and bottling house, but the remaining Powerhouse is a great example of brewery architecture at the turn of the last century. Designed by architect Hugh Garden, this remaining building illustrates a dramatic shift in architectural taste. Entrance to the Powerhouse is through a massive square-arched doorway, with the company name incised in the Bedford limestone. Thick brick piers and recessed windows make this horizontal building seem taller than it is.

The Powerhouse's Prairie style relies on a bold organization of facades and ornamental brickwork for its visual impact. The building's strong, modern, horizontal lines are somewhat akin to what Frank Lloyd Wright had done in residential styles.

The last buildings on the site were built in 1912. Schoenhofen ceased brewing during Prohibition, closing in 1924. The building was converted to grain warehousing. This building and the other remaining, Victorian-style ornamented Administration Building next door, were threatened with demolition in the 1980s. It was made a Chicago Landmark in July 1988.

P-SCHOENHOFEN BREWING CO
500

210 South Canal Street

UNION STATION

1913–25: Graham, Anderson, Probst & White

Step into the past, into one of the nation's grand train stations, when railroad travel was the only way to go and stations were as beautiful and comfortable as possible. Step also into the present, in the country's third-busiest railway terminal. Union Station is both—an early-20th-century elegant, luxurious waiting space today used by the racing, pacing, often hassled, 21st-century rail travelers.

Railroads made Chicago great. Being the nation's railroad capital meant the city grew with dozens of lines coming into Chicago from all directions. Union Station consisted, when first built, of two main parts: a large waiting room in an office building on the west side and a concourse on the east. The concourse was demolished in 1969. But the exquisite waiting room still exists in what is the last remaining great railroad terminal built when Chicago reigned as the undisputed rail center of the US.

The Great Hall, as the waiting room is called, is one of the grandest interior spaces in the city. Designed in Neo-Classical or Beaux Arts style, which brings a great deal of ornamentation, the room is lined in travertine marble Corinthian columns. A 219-foot barrel-vaulted skylight soars 115 feet over the room. Two statues tower over the Great Hall on the east wall. Henry Hering, sculptor, created the rooster representing "day" and the owl signifying "night." The light torchiers have birds, bees, and butterflies feasting on flowers. While the floor has been called pink marble, geologically it is really compact limestone.

The exterior of the station is clad in Bedford limestone, highlighted by rows of Doric columns, another example of Neo-Classical design.

The station, designated a Chicago Landmark in May 2002, has been featured in many movies and TV shows over the years.

601 South Morgan Street

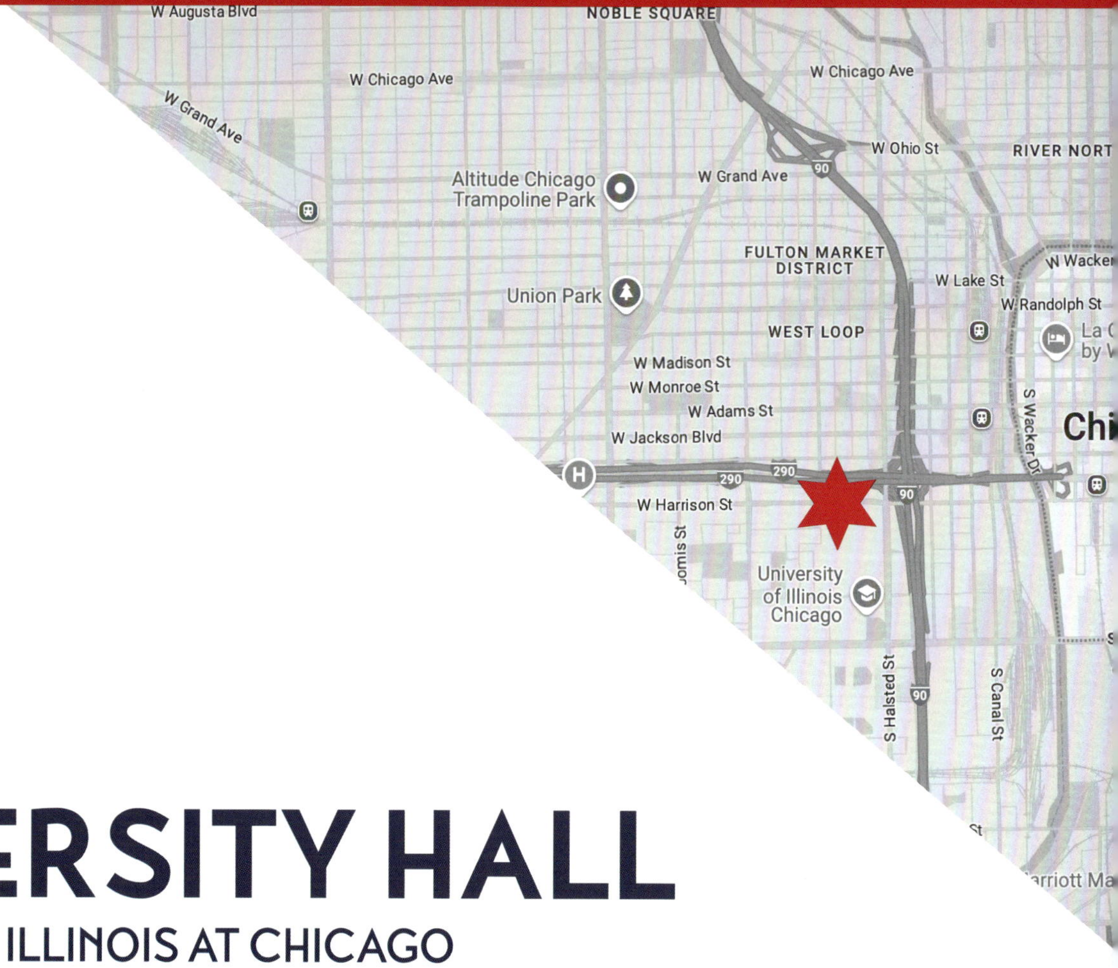

UNIVERSITY HALL

UNIVERSITY OF ILLINOIS AT CHICAGO

1965-67: Skidmore, Owings & Merrill, Walter Netsch, architect

The University of Illinois at Chicago didn't begin at this site. Its first iteration was a two-year University of Illinois undergraduate extension program for returning World War II veterans, located on Navy Pier. The popularity of "Harvard on the Rocks," as the school was jokingly called, was a major impetus for establishing UIC, the city's largest university serving more than 33,500 undergraduate, graduate, and professional students. SOM was chosen to design the entire campus, and project architect Walter Netsch opted for the then-popular Brutalist style, which was considered revolutionary.

The result, according to some, was one of the most hated school architecture styles ever. UIC has since constructed many other buildings that "hide" or reduce the impact of its Brutalist beginnings. Nevertheless, this building stands out—both physically and metaphorically.

Brutalism, a worldwide style popular particularly for public buildings in the decades following World War II, features exposed structural elements and strong materials like concrete, brick, and granite. Netsch created a campus plan based on the metaphor of a stone dropped in a pond. Buildings were grouped by function, with the most important forming a close circle in the center.

University Hall, an office tower on the campus's north side, is the tallest on campus and its most visible symbol. Intended as a landmark—some say a metaphorical campanile or bell tower—the building is composed of reinforced concrete (concrete that has steel embedded in it) with narrow recessed windows. The 28-story building gets bigger as it rises, from 150 feet wide at the bottom, growing to 160 feet wide for floors 8 to 16 and 170 feet wide above. Enormous columns at ground level support the weight.

The university may have tried to hide it, but it is the campus's Brutalist base that gives it its character.

Union Station

SOURCES

INTRODUCTION

https://www.dezeen.com/2024/09/05/chicago-skyscrapers-recently-completed/

https://ultimatetraveladvice.com/slideshow/destinations/the-windy-city-top-15-things-you-can't-miss-in-chicago

IN THE LOOP

1. 135 South LaSalle Street (Field Building)

   Bach, Ira. *Chicago on Foot: An Architecture Walking Tour.* Chicago: Follett Publishing Co. 1969.

   Jones Lang LaSalle, Inc. "The LaSalle Bank Building," promotional brochure.

2. 403 South State Street (2nd Leiter Bldg.)

   "Second Leiter Building." Chicago: City of Chicago Commission on Chicago Historical and Architectural Landmarks, 1978.

3. 820 South (Johnson Publishing Company)

   Press release. "Mayor Rahm Emanuel Announces Johnson Publishing Building to Be Considered for Landmark Status." Feb. 2, 2017.

4. Aon Center

   https://www/,sm/cp,em-us/money/realestate/ranked-america-s-25-tallest-skyscrapers/ss-AA1oxyDW#interstitial=3

   Bosch, Jennifer Marjorie. *A View from the River: The Chicago Architecture Foundation River Cruise.* Portland, OR: Pomegranate, 2008.

5. Aqua

   Belogolovsky, Vladimir. *Architectural Guide Chicago: A Critic's Guide to 100 Post-Modern Buildings in Chicago from 1978 to 2025.* Berlin: DOM Publishers, 2022.

   Chicago Architecture Center and John Hill. *Guide to Chicago's Twenty-First-Century Architecture.* Urbana: University of Illinois Press.

6. ARC @ Old Colony Building

   https://chicagology.com/goldenage/goldenage137/

7. Art Institute of Chicago

   https://www.artic.edu/artworks/656/lion-one-of-pair-south-pedestal

   Phipps, Linda S. "The 1893 Art Institute Building and the 'Paris of America': Aspiration of Patrons and Architects in Late 19th Century Chicago." *Art Institute of Chicago Museum Studies,* Vol. 14, No. 1 (1988), pp. 28-45, 99-102.

8. Art Institute of Chicago Modern Wing

   https://www/archdaily.com/24653/the-modern-wing-renzo-piano

   Belogolovsky, Vladimir. *Architectural Guide: Chicago: A Critic's Guide to 100 Post-Modern Buildings in Chicago from 1978 to 2025.* Berlin: DOM Publishers. 2022.

9. Auditorium (Theatre) Building

   https://www.msn.com/en-US/travel/news/32-most-famous-buildings-in-chicago/

   Schulze, Franz and Kevin Harrington. *Chicago's Famous Buildings: Fourth Edition/Revised and Enlarged.* Chicago: The University of Chicago Press, 1993.

10. Chicago Athletic Association Hotel

    https://www.architecture.org/online-resources/buildings-of-chicago/chicago-athletic-association-hotel

    https://savingplaces.org/stories/inside-the-chicago-athletic-club-hotel

11. Chicago Board of Trade

    "Chicago Board of Trade Building." Chicago: Commission on Chicago Historical and Architectural Landmarks, Aug. 1975.

12. Chicago Cultural Center

    https://msn.com/en-us/travel/tripideas/53-awesome-hidden-gems-in-chicago-that-are-worth-visiting/ar-BB1qkXOo

    https://www.msn.com/en-us/arts-visiual-art-and-design/high-art-the-world-s-most-incredible-ceilings/ss/bb102vcR

    Schulze, Franz and Kevin Harrington, Eds. *Chicago's Famous Buildings: A Photographic Guide to the City's Architectural Landmarks and Other Notable Buildings, 4th Ed.* Chicago: University of Chicago Press, 1993.

13. Chicago Federal Center

    https://architecture.org/online-resources/building-of-chicago/federal-center

    https://www.gsa.gov/about-us/gsa-regions/region-5-great-lakes/buildings-and-facilities/illinois/chicago-kluczynski-fb-loop-uspo

    https://www.wttw.com/loop/buildings/chicago-federal-center

14. Daley Center

    https://webapps/chicago.gov/landmarksweb/web/landmarkdetails.htm?lanld=1285&counter=77

    Bach, Ira J. *Chicago on Foot: An Architectural Walking Tour.* Chicago: Follett Publishing Co., 1969.

15. Fisher Building

    "Fisher Building." Chicago: City of Chicago Commission on Chicago Historical and Architectural Landmarks, 1983.

16. Harold Washington Library Center

    https://www.architecture.org/online/resources/buildings-of-chicago/harold-washington-library

17. Inland Steel Building

    https://www.architecture.org/online/resources/buildings-of-chicago/inland-steel

    https://webapps/chicago.gov/landmarksweb/web/landmarkdetails.htm?lanld=1336&counter=160

    https://www.nbc.chicago.com/local/inland_steel_other_local_sites_put_on_the_historic_register_//873278/

18. Marquette Building

    Berger, Miles L. "Office Towers: Owen F. Aldis (1953-1925)." *They Built Chicago: Entrepreneurs Who Shaped a Great City's Architecture.* Chicago: Bonus Books Inc., 1992, pp. 39-48.

    Derderian, Kevork. "National Landmark, The Marquette Building, Receives Renovations During Its Centennial Year." Chicago: *Realty and Building/The REHAB Market,* April 29, 1995.

    "The Marquette Building." Quarter fold brochure issued by the John D. and Catherine T. MacArthur Foundation.

19. Metropolitan Correctional Center

    https://www.blueprintchicago.org/2010/12/22/metropolitan-correctional-center

20. Monadnock Building

    Salvia, Vanessa. "The Monadnock Building: A History With Masonry." https://masonrymagazine.com/

    https://www.msn.com/en-us/travel/tripideas/53-awesome-hidden-gems-in-chicago-worth-visiting/ar-BBlqkxoo

    "Summary of Information on the Monadnock Building." Chicago: City of Chicago Commission on Chicago Historical and Architectural Landmarks, April 30, 1970.

    Walsh, Michelle Byrne. "Monadnock Block was built to last forever and has 100 years to prove it." *Dodge Construction News,* Jan. 22, 1991.

21. Orchestra Hall at Symphony Center

    Schulze, Franz and Kevin Harrington, Eds. *Chicago's Famous Buildings: A Photographic Guide to the City's Architectural Landmarks and Other Notable Buildings.* Chicago: University of Chicago Press, 4th Ed., 1993.

22. Pendry Hotel (Carbide and Carbon Building)

    https://www.insidechicagowalkingtour.com/blog/20202/3/31/art-deco-glam.the-carbide-and-carbon-building

23. Spertus Institute

    https://www.architecture.org/online-resources/buildings-of-chicago/spertus-institute

    https://www.spertus.edu/about-our-building

    Belogolovsky, Vladimir. *Architectural Guide: Chicago: A Critic's Guide to 100 Post-Modern Buildings in Chicago from 1978 to 2025.* Berlin: DOM Publishers, 2022.

24. Staypineapple Hotel (Reliance Building)

https://www.architecture.org/online-resources/buildings-of-chicago/reliance-building

25. Sullivan Center

"Carson Pirie Scott & Company Building." Chicago: City of Chicago Commission on Chicago Historical and Architectural Landmarks, 1978.

Bach, Ira J. *Chicago on Foot: An Architectural Walking Tour*. Chicago: Follett Publishing Co., 1969.

26. The Rookery

"The Rookery." Commission on Chicago Historical and Architectural Landmarks. Chicago: City of Chicago, 1979.

27. Thompson Center

https://blog.google/inside-google/life-at-google-google-chicago-office-thompson-center/

28. US Bank Building (190 South LaSalle Street)

Belogolovsky, Vladimir. *Architectural Guide: Chicago: A Critic's Guide to 100 Post-Modern Buildings in Chicago from 1978 to 2025.* Berlin: DOM Publishers, 2022.

Gregerson, John. "Classicism and Commerce Converge on LaSalle Street." *Building Design & Construction*, March 1988.

ON THE RIVER

29. 150 North Riverside Plaza

https://riversideid.com

Bosch, Jennifer Marjorie. *A View from the River: The Chicago Architecture Foundation River Cruise.* Portland, OR: Pomegranate Communications Inc., 2008.

Riverside Investments and Development; Goettsch Partners. "150 North Riverside, Chicago Illinois," promotional brochure. rivesideid.com; gpchicago.com

30. 333 West Wacker Drive

Bosch, Jennifer Marjorie. *A View from the River: The Chicago Architecture Foundation River Cruise.* Portland, OR: Pomegranate Communications Inc., 2008.

31. AMA Plaza

https://www.architecture.org/online-resources/buildings-of-chicago-/330-north-wabash-ama-plaza-ibm-plaza

32. Apple Michigan Avenue Store

https://www.architecture.org/online-resources/buildings-of-chicago/apple-michigan-avenue

https://www/dezeem/com/2017/10/20/apple-store-michigan-avenue-foster-partners-chicago-riverfront-macbook-shaped-roof/

33. Civic Opera House

https://webapps/chicago.gov/landmarksweb/web/landmarkdetails.htm?lanld=1278&counter=67

34. Lake Point Tower

https://www.youtube.com/lakeposinttower

35. London House

https://www.architecture.org/online-resources/buildings-of-chicago/london-guarantee-building?

https://livinglandmarksofchicago.com/londonhouse-hotel

Bizzarri, Amy. *111 Places in Chicago That You Must Not Miss.* Dortmund, Germany: Emons Verlag GmbH, 2017.

36. Marina City

https://www.marinacity.org

37. Old Post Office

https://www.chicago.gov/city/en/depts/dcd/provdrs/hist/news/2018/january/landmark-designation-proposed-for-old-main-post-office-buidling.htm

38. River Point

Belogolovsky, Vladimir. *Architectural Guide: Chicago: A Critic's Guide to 100 Post-Modern Buildings in Chicago from 1978 to 2025.* Berlin: DOM Publishers, 2022.

Chicago Architecture Center and John Hill. *Guide to Chicago's Twenty-first Century Architecture.* Urbana: University of Illinois Press, 2021.

39. St. Regis Chicago

Belogolovsky, Vladimir. *Architectural Guide Chicago: A Critic's Guide to 100 Post-Modern Buildings in Chicago from 1978 to 2025.* Berlin: DOM Publishers, 2022, pp. 52-3.

Chicago Architecture Center and John Hill. *Guide to Chicago's Twenty-First Century Architecture.* Urbana: University of Illinois Press, 2021.

40. The Mart

https://www.bloomberg.com/news/features/2024-08-10/chicago-s-art-deco-merchandise-mart-reborn-as-21st-century-office-space

Byrnes, Mark. "How Chicago's Gigantic Merchandise Mart Is Still Thriving as Office Space." New York: Bloomberg News, Aug. 10. 2024.

41. Tribune Tower Residences

https://www.msn.com/en-us/travel/news/32-most-famous-buildings-in-chicago/arAA1vU4mW?ocid=msedgdhp&pc=LSJS&cvid=907881889a3a49b78d51d447a630a5bb&ei=13

https://buildingsdb.com/IL/chicago/chicago-tribune-tower

42. Trump International Hotel and Tower

https://www.ranker.com/list/tallest-buidlings-in-Chicago/ranker-travel

Bosch, Jennifer Marjorie. *A View from the River: The Chicago Architecture Foundation River Cruise.* Portland, OR: Pomegranate, 2008.

43. Willis Tower

Bosch, Jennifer Marjorie. *A View from the River: The Chicago Architecture Foundation River Cruise.* Portland, OR: Pomegranate, 2008.

44. Wrigley Building

http://www.thewrigleybuilding.com/fun-facts/

https://www.chicago.gov/content/dam/city/depts/zlup/Historic_Preservation_Publications/Wrigley_Building.pdf

NORTH SIDE

45. 860-880 North Lake Shore Drive

https://860880lakeshoredrive.com/chicago-landmark-award-for-preservation-excellence-2010/

https://buildingsdb.com/IL/chicago/860-880-lake-shore-dirve-apartments/

46. 875 North Michigan Avenue, John Hancock Building

https://skyscrapersworld.com/us-tallest-skyscrapers

Museum of Science and Industry. *A Guide to 150 Years of Chicago Architecture.* Chicago: Chicago Review Press, 1985.

47. Carl Schurz High School

https://www.schurzhs.org/apps/pages/index.jsp?uREC_ID=235490&type=d&pREC_ID=468563

https://www.chicago.gov/city/en/dataset/indivudal_landmarks.html

Schulze, Franz and Kevin Harrington. *Chicago's Famous Buildings*. Chicago: The University of Chicago Press, 1993.

48. Charnley-Persky House

Drury, John. *Old Chicago Houses*. Chicago: The University of Chicago Press, 1975.

Schulze, Franz and Kevin Harrington, Eds. *Chicago's Famous Buildings: A Photographic Guide to the City's Architectural Landmarks and Other Notable Buildings, 4th Ed.* Chicago: University of Chicago Press, 1993.

49. Elks Memorial Building

https://www.elkd.org/memorial/memorialTour/cfn

https://webapps/chicago.gov/landmarksweb/web/landmarkdetails.htm?lanld=1545&counter=95

50. Independence Apartments and Branch Library

Belogolovsky, Vladimir. *Architectural Guide: Chicago: A Critic's Guide to 100 Post-Modern Buildings in Chicago from 1978 to 2025.* Berlin: DOM Publishers, 2022.

Chicago Architecture Center and John Hill. *Guide to Chicago's Twenty-first Century Architecture.* Chicago: Board of Trustees, University of Illinois, 2021.

51. McDonald's Flagship

https://www./r-barc.com/work/mcdonalds-global-flagship-chicago

Shubart, Ellen. *What's With Chicago? The quirks, personality, and charm of the Windy City*. St. Louis: Reedy Press, 2018.

52. NEIL El Centro Campus

https://news.wttw.com/2014/10/06/blair-kamin-el-centro-god-box

https://www.archdaily.com/963374/northeastern-illinois-university-jgma

53. Poetry Foundation

https://www.architecture.org/online-resources/buildings-of-chicago/poetry-foundation

54. United Airlines Terminal One

Belogolovsky, Vladimir. *Architectural Guide: Chicago: A Critic's Guide to 100 Post-Modern Buildings in Chicago from 1978 to 2025*. Berlin: DOM Publishers, 2022.

Sirefman, Susanna. *Chicago: A guide to recent architecture.* London: Ellippis London Limited, 1996.

55. Water Tower

Hogan, John F. *The Chicago Water Tower.* Charleston, SC: The History Press, 2019.

56. Wrigley Field

Shubart, Ellen. *What's With Chicago? The quirks, personality, and charm of the Windy City*. St. Louis: Reedy Press, 2018.

57. Yannell Net-Zero Energy Residence

https://www.farrside.com/yanell-house

SOUTH SIDE

58. Booth School of Business

https://www.vinoly.com/works/univesoty-of-chicago-booth-school-of-business-charles-m-harper-center/

https://architecture.uchicago.edulocations/charles_m._parker_center

59. Chicago Bungalow

https://www.ChicagoBungalowAssociation.org

https://www.chicagobungalow.org/current-bungalow-historic-districts

Sonoc, Scott. "Defining the Chicago Bungalow." *The Chicago Bungalow*. Chicago: Chicago Architecture Foundation, 2003.

60. Chicago Public Library, Chicago Bee Branch

https://sagecollective.org/a-brief-history-of-the-chicago-bee

https://www.nps/gpv/places/bronzeville-black-metropolis-national-heritage-area.htm

https://webapps/chicago.gov/landmarks/web/landmarkdetails.htm?landid=1268

Bey, Lee. *Southern Exposure: The Overlooked Architecture of Chicago's South Side.* Evanston, IL: Northwestern University Press, 2019.

61. Chicago Public Library Chinatown Branch

https://www.chipublib.org./about-chinatown-branch/

https://www.architecture.org/open-house-chicago/sites/recRNhxrPCE8R-cWE3

62. Crown Hall

Michelin Tourist Guide: Chicago. Ft. Worth, TX: Michelin et Cie, Proprietaires Editeurs, 1996.

Schulze, Franz. "American Apogee: Commercial and Institutional Work, 1950–1959." *Mies, a Critical Biography*. Chicago: The University of Chicago Press, 2012, pp. 304–313.

63. Ed Kaplan Family Institute for Innovation and Tech Entrepreneurship

https://www.archdaily.com/911217/ed-kaplan-family-institute-john-ronan-architects

https://www.world-arhcitects.com/en/architecture-news/reviews/ed-kaplan-family-institute-for-innovation-and-tech-entrepreneurship

https://chicago.curbed.com/2018/11/1/18022746/iit-kaplan-institute-innovation-center-john-roran

64. Glessner House

https://travelpug.net/19-historical-spots-in-Chicago-that-most-tourists-miss/

Bizzarri, Amy. *111 Places in Chicago That You Must Not Miss.* Germany: Emons Verlag GmbH, 2017.

Drury, John. *Old Chicago Homes*. Chicago: University of Chicago Press, 1975.

Siegel, Arthur, Ed. *Chicago's Famous Buildings: a photogenic guide.* Chicago: The University of Chicago Press, 1965.

65. Griffin Museum of Science and Industry

https://www.architecture.org/online-resources/buildings-of-chicago/museum-of-science-and-industry

https://webapps1.chicago.gov./landmarksweb/web/landmarkdetails.htm?lanid=1376

Bey, Lee. *Southern Exposure: The Overlooked Architecture of Chicago's South Side*. Evanston, IL: Northwestern University Press, 2019.

66. Hilliard Towers Apartments

https://docomomo-us.org/register/hilliard-tower-apartments

67. Illinois Tech McCormick Tribune Campus Center

Belogolovsky, Vladimir. *Architectural Guide: Chicago: A Critic's Guide to 100 Post-Modern Buildings in Chicago from 1978 to 2025.* Berlin: DOM Publishers, 2022.

Chicago Architecture Center and John Hill. *Guide to Chicago's Twenty-first Century Architecture*. Chicago: Board of Trustees, University of Illinois, 2021.

68. Joe and Rika Mansueto Library

https://www.chicagotribune.com/2011/05/18/for-books-new-life-in-a-bubble/

Belogolovsky, Vladimir. *Architectural Guide: Chicago: A Critic's Guide to 100 Post-Modern Buildings in Chicago from 1978 to 2025.* Berlin: DOM Publishers, 2022.

Bjone, Christian. *I Love Chicago's Buildings: A selective guide to the city*. China: ORO Editions, 2022.

69. Lakeside Technology Center

https://www.equinx.com/data-centers

Siegel, Arthur, Ed. *Chicago's Famous Buildings: a photographic guide.* Chicago: University of Chicago Press, 1965.

70. Obama Presidential Center

Bey, Lee. *Southern Exposure: The Overlooked Architecture of Chicago's South Side.* Evanston, IL: Northwestern University Press, 2019.

Chicago Architecture Center and John Hill. *Guide to Chicago's Twenty-first Century Architecture*. Chicago: Board of Trustees, University of Illinois, 2021.

71. Pui Tak Center

https://www.wttw.com/most-beautiful-places-in-chicago/dramatic-architecture/pui-tak-center

https:/www.puitak.org/building

72. Pullman Historic District

https://ultimatetraveladvice.com/slideshow/destinations/the-windy-city-top-15-things-you-cant-miss-in-chicago

https://www.pullmanil.org/clock-tower-and-adminsitration-building

Bey, Lee. *Southern Exposure: The Overlooked Architecture of Chicago's South Side.* Evanston, IL: Northwestern University Press, 2019.

Siegel, Arthur, Ed. *Chicago's Famous Buildings: a photographic guide.* Chicago: The University of Chicago Press, 1965.

73. Robie House

Birk, Melanie. *Frank Lloyd Wright and the Prairie*. New York: Universe Publishing, 1998.

Drury, John. *Old Chicago Houses*. Chicago: The University of Chicago Press, 1975.

74. Rosenwald Garden Apartments

https://www/thecha.org/rosenwald-courts-pbv

Bey, Lee. *Southern Exposure: The Overlooked Architecture of Chicago's South Side.* Evanston, IL: Northwestern University Press, 2019.

75. South Shore Culture Center

https://www.chicago.gov/content/dam/city/depts/zlup/Historic_Preservation/Publications/South_Shore_Cultural_Center

Peterson, Laurie McGovern, ed. *AIA Guide to Chicago, 4th Ed.* Chicago: AIA Chicago and the Guide to Chicago Architecture Joint Venture, 2002.

WEST SIDE

76. 800 Fulton Market

https://800fultonmarket.com

Belogolovsky, Vladimir. *Architectural Guide: Chicago: A Critic's Guide to 100 Post-Modern Buildings in Chicago from 1978 to 2025.* Berlin: DOM Publishers. 2022

77. Garfield Park Conservatory

https://travelpug.net/19-historical-spots-in-Chicago-that-most-tourists-miss/

Bizzarri, Amy. *111 Places in Chicago That You Must Not Miss.* Dortmund, Germany: Emons Verlag GmbH, 2017.

78. Old Cook County Hospital

https://www.archdaily.com/948788/som-transforms-chicagos-100-year-old-cook-county-hospital

https://www.nps.gov./articles/cook-county-hospital.htm

https://www/chicago.gov/city/en/depts/dcd/provdrs/hist/news/2019/december/former-cook-county-hospital-proposed-for-landmark-status.html

https://www.;andmarks.or/old-cook-county-hospital-rehabilitated/

https://www.walshgroup.com/news/2021/renovationoftheoldcookcountyhospitalbuildingisnamedmidwestprojectoftheyear.html/

79. Chicago Park District Headquarters

https://www.chicagoparkdistrict.comn/parks-facilities/brighton-park-coummunity-campus-park-no-596

https://www.archdaily.com/1018959/chicago-park-district-headquarters-and-fieldhouse-john-ronan-architects

80. Schoenhofen Brewery

https://webapps1.chicago.gov/landmarksweb/web/home.htm

https://forgottenchicago.com/articles/schoenhofen-brewery

https://webapps1.chicago.gov./landmarksweb/web/architectdetails.htm?arcid-13

81. Union Station

https://www.architecture.org/online-resources/buildings-of-chicago/union-station

Museum of Science and Industry. *A Guide to 150 Years of Chicago Architecture.* Chicago: Chicago Review Press, 1985

82. University Hall

https://studylib.net/doc/8279002/introducing-the-historic-netsch-campus-at-uic

https://www/uic.edu

BOOKS

Bach, Ira J. *Chicago on Foot: An Architectural Walking Tour*. Chicago: Follett Publishing Co., 1969.

Belogolovsky, Vladimir. *Architectural Guide: Chicago: A Critic's Guide to 100 Post-Modern Buildings in Chicago from 1978 to 2025.* Berlin: DOM Publishers, 2022.

Bey, Lee. *Southern Exposure: The Overlooked Architecture of Chicago's South Side.* Evanston, IL: Northwestern University Press, 2019.

Bizzarri, Amy. *111 Places in Chicago That You Must Not Miss.* Dortmund, Germany: Emons Verlag GmbH, 2017.

Bjone, Christian. *I Love Chicago's Buildings: A selective guide to the city*. China: ORO Editions, 2022.

Bosch, Jennifer Marjorie. *A View from the River: the Chicago Architecture Foundation River Cruise.* Portland, OR: Pomegranate, 2008.

Chicago Architecture Center and John Hill. *Guide to Chicago's Twenty-first Century Architecture*. Chicago: Board of Trustees, University of Illinois, 2021.

Drury, John. *Old Chicago Houses*. Chicago: The University of Chicago Press, 1975.

McBrien, Judith Paine. *Pocket Guide to Chicago Architecture.* New York: W. W. Norton & Co., 1997.

Peterson, Laurie McGovern, ed. *AIA Guide to Chicago, 4th Ed.* Chicago: AIA Chicago and the Guide to Chicago Architecture Joint Venture, 2002.

Schulze, Franz and Kevin Harrington, eds. *Chicago's Famous Buildings: A Photographic Guide to the City's Architectural Landmarks and Other Notable Buildings, 4th Ed.* Chicago: University of Chicago Press, 1993.

Shubart, Ellen. *What's With Chicago? The quirks, personality, and charm of the Windy City.* St. Louis: Reedy Press, 2018.

Siegel, Arthur, ed. *Chicago's Famous Buildings: a photographic guide.* Chicago: The University of Chicago Press, 1965.

Sirefman, Susanna. *Chicago: A guide to recent architecture.* London: Ellippis London Limited, 1996.

INDEX